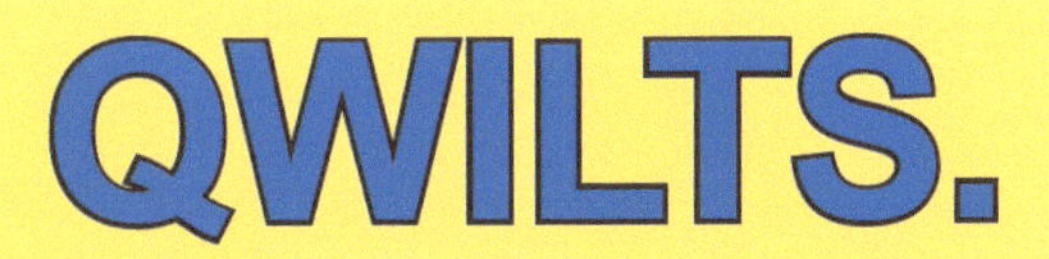

LEARN TO MAKE GRAFFITI TAG MINI QUILTS

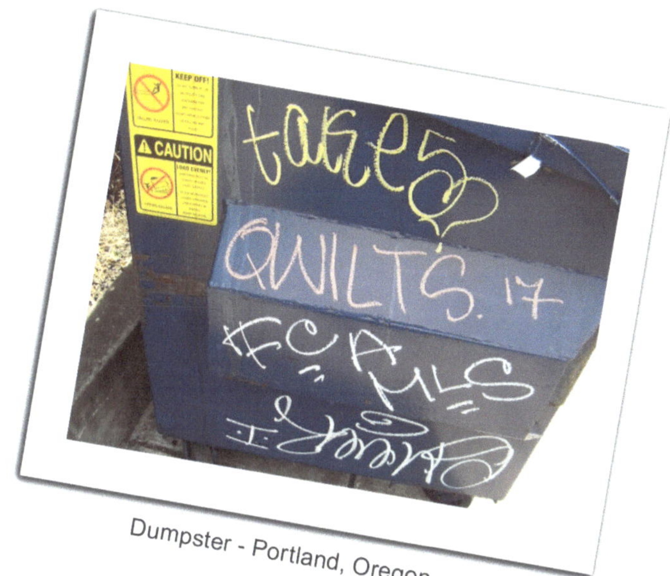

Dumpster - Portland, Oregon

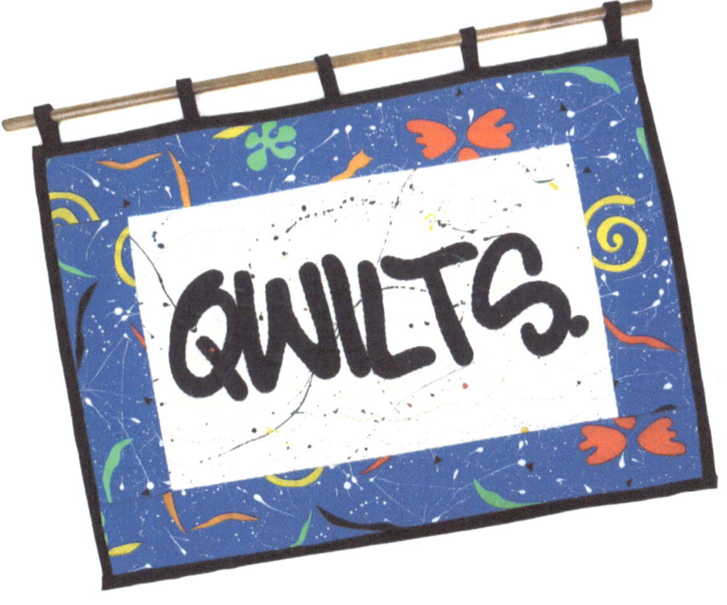

Be an entrepreneur, not a vandal. Put your graffiti tags on hand-made products you can sell like these super, awesome mini quilts. Don't get arrested, get paid!

CONTENTS

Dedicated to SOUNDGARDEN

Thank you for the music!

In Memory of Chris Cornell

This book derives its name from the graffiti tag, QWILTS, which I found on a dumpster and photographed in Portland, Oregon.

QWILTS. LEARN TO MAKE GRAFFITI TAG MINI QUILTS
First Printing, 2017
ISBN-13: 978-0-9904381-7-5
ISBN-10: 0-9904381-7-1
Published By Graffiti Diplomacy
All illustrations, photographs, text, and cover art produced by Graffiti Diplomacy
For general information on our other products and services, please contact us at "graffitidiplomacy@yahoo.com"

Special thanks to Dr. Leonard Deutsch, Stephen Spiegel, and to Xanaland Blog, which has been an inspiration.
Find us on the web @ graffitidiplomacy.com

INTRODUCTION

It was a warm summer day in the Pacific Northwest and I was sitting on a bench at the station waiting for my train. I was leaning forward, concentrating intensely on sewing the border of a graffiti tag mini quilt. A girl sat down beside me on the bench, about 18 years old. “Can I see what you are making?” she asked politely. “Sure,” I said and held up the quilt for her to see. Her eyes opened wide in amazement and she said, “Wow, I didn’t know you could do that with graffiti?” I said, “Well, that’s because I made it up.” “My boyfriend does graffiti,” she said. “We love graffiti!” I replied, “I am from New York and I have traveled around the country taking pictures of thousands of graffiti tags. Sometimes I put them into mini quilts like this one and sometimes I design my own tags to use in these quilts. There are lots of great things you can do with graffiti that are perfectly legal. And better still, I can sell this mini quilt and make money!” “Thanks,” she said with a smile. She totally got my concept! I knew I was onto something big. Just then the train pulled in and we went our separate ways.

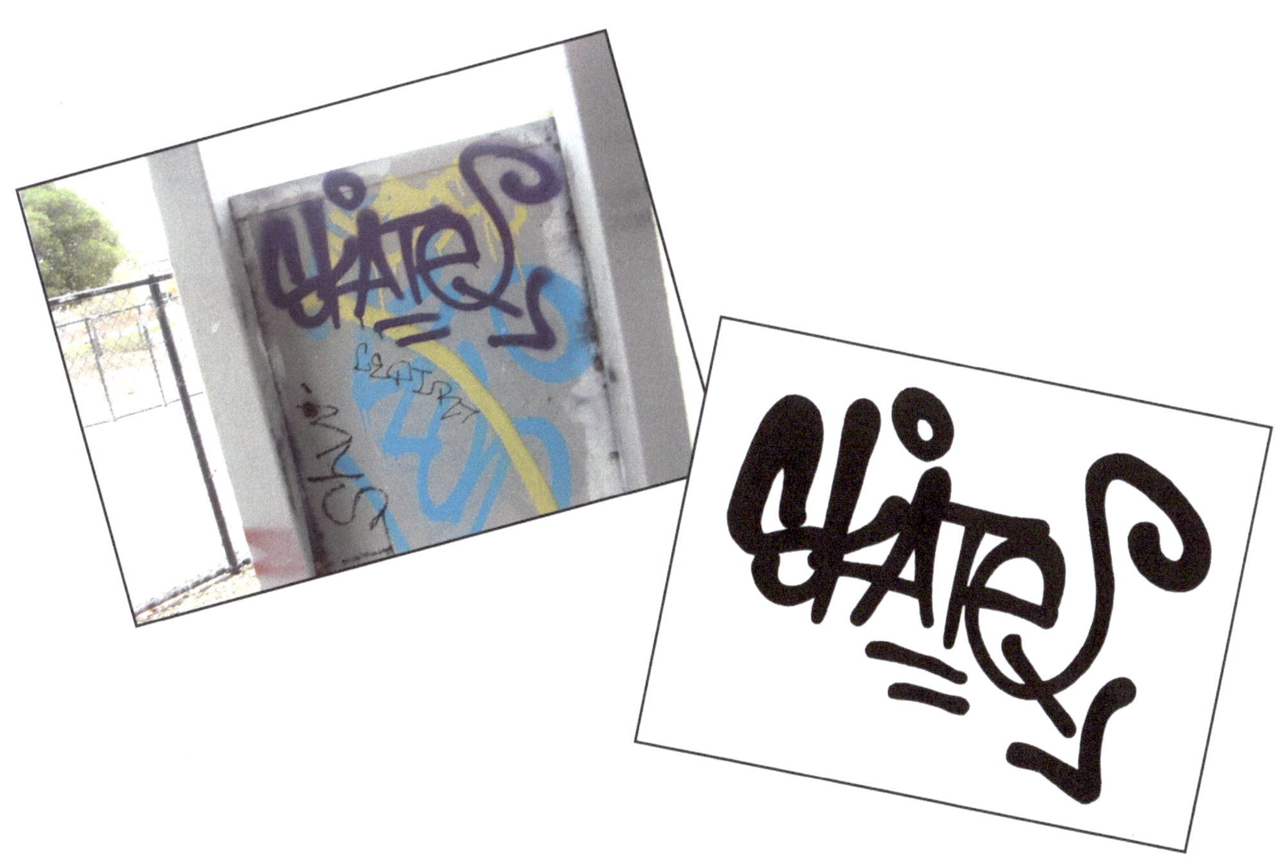

“I love it when a plan comes together.” - The A-Team

ABOUT THIS BOOK

This is a book for people who see magic in a graffiti tag scrawled on a mailbox or a dumpster. People who, instead of seeing tags as vandalism, want to draw graffiti tags as art but in a way that is legal. Also, this book offers a new perspective on the old art form of quilting. It's for people who want to explore the possibilities of combining traditional fiber art with contemporary street art style. And finally, this book is for people who want to create one-of-a-kind or reproducible handmade products they can sell.

You can use just about any tag to make a mini quilt. Tags with stylish looking letters and interesting features such as arrows, curlicues or halos can make great quilts. Look at the examples in this book for inspiration, then why not try your hand at designing your own tags to use in your quilts?

If you want to design your own tags, our two instructional books, "Learn to Draw a Graffiti Master-Piece," and "Why Write When You Can Tag: Learn To Draw The Best Graffiti Tags Ever!" are a great place to learn tagging and lettering techniques.

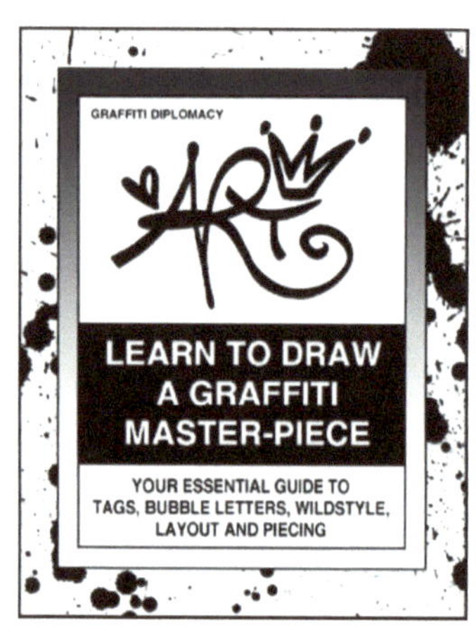

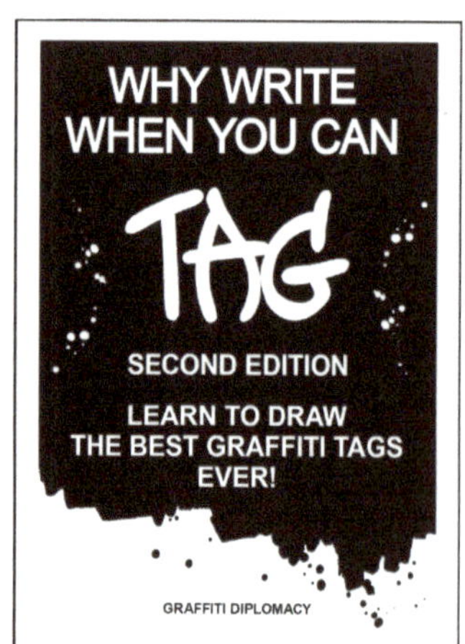

If you decide to photograph and experiment with other people's tags, be safe, be respectful of others' work, and never use gang graffiti in your quilts. Instructions for making the quilts can be found starting on Page 40. Whether it's for fun or profit, making graffiti tag mini quilts is a fast and easy way to create something totally unique. Maybe even a little subversive ;)

ABOUT THOSE FINISHED QUILT SIZES

A mini quilt can be any size you want it to be. I have included the finished size for each quilt in the descriptions beneath the photographs, but these sizes are completely random. When people ask me how big a mini quilt should be I say, "Smaller than a pillowcase, bigger than half a pillowcase."

WHAT YOU WILL NEED

These are just some suggestions. Feel free to improvise in whatever way is needed.

DRAWING AND PAINTING SUPPLIES

#2 Pencil & Sharpener
Magic Markers
Ruler
Fabric Paint
Paint Brushes

<u>NOT SHOWN:</u>
Drawing Paper
Clear Contact Paper
Masking Tape or Blue Tape
Cardboard or Canvas Board
Acrylic Paint and Varnish

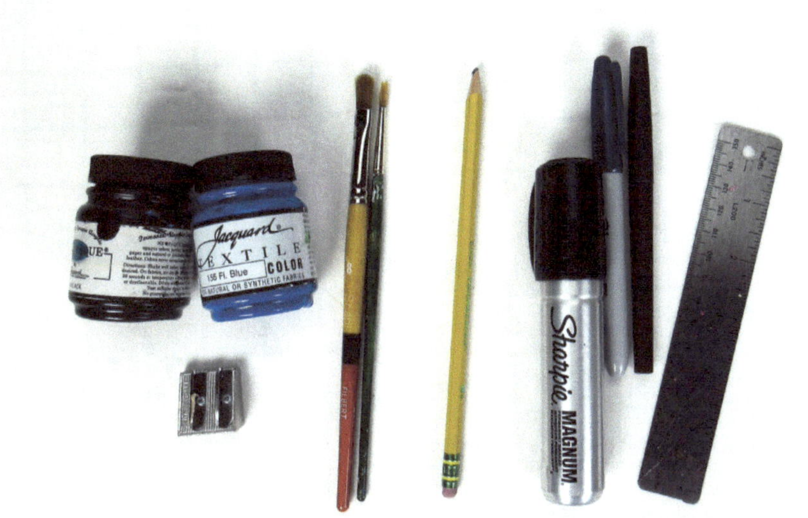

SEWING SUPPLIES

Quilter's Hoop
Assorted Sewing Threads
Quilting Needles
Pincushion
Tape Measure
Safety Pins
Thimble
Water-Erasable Pencil
Needle Threader
Scissors & Cutting Wheel
Seam Ripper

<u>NOT SHOWN:</u>
Cotton Fabrics
Quilt Batting - Thin
Double-Fold,
Extra-Wide Bias Tape
Iron or Clothes Dryer
Wooden Dowel

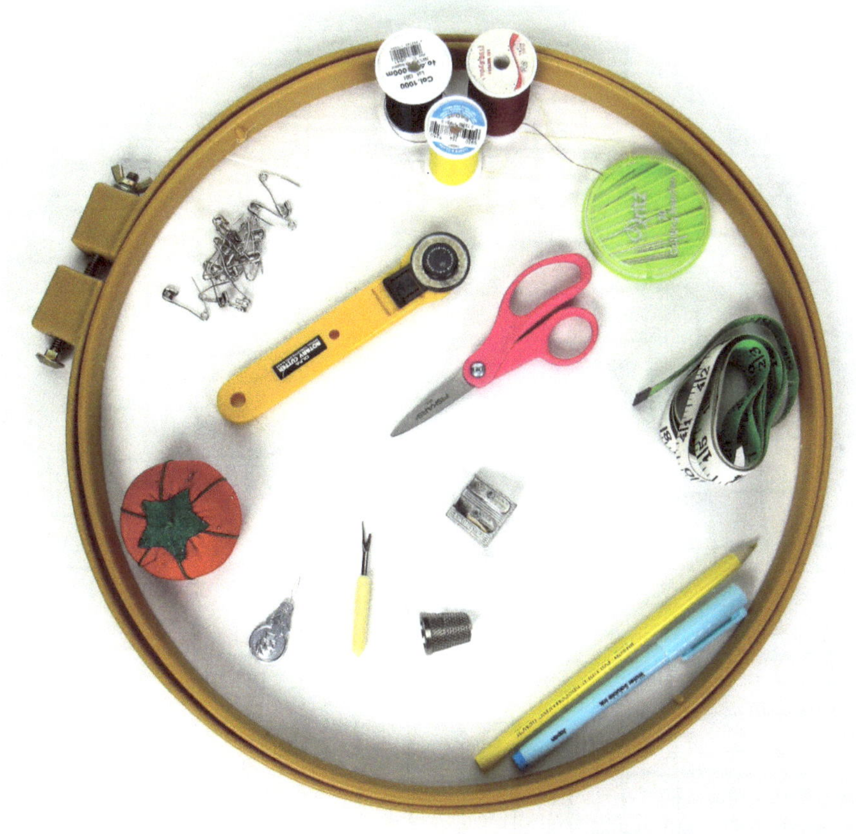

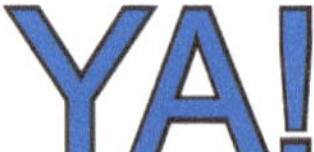

Construction Container - Manhattan, New York City

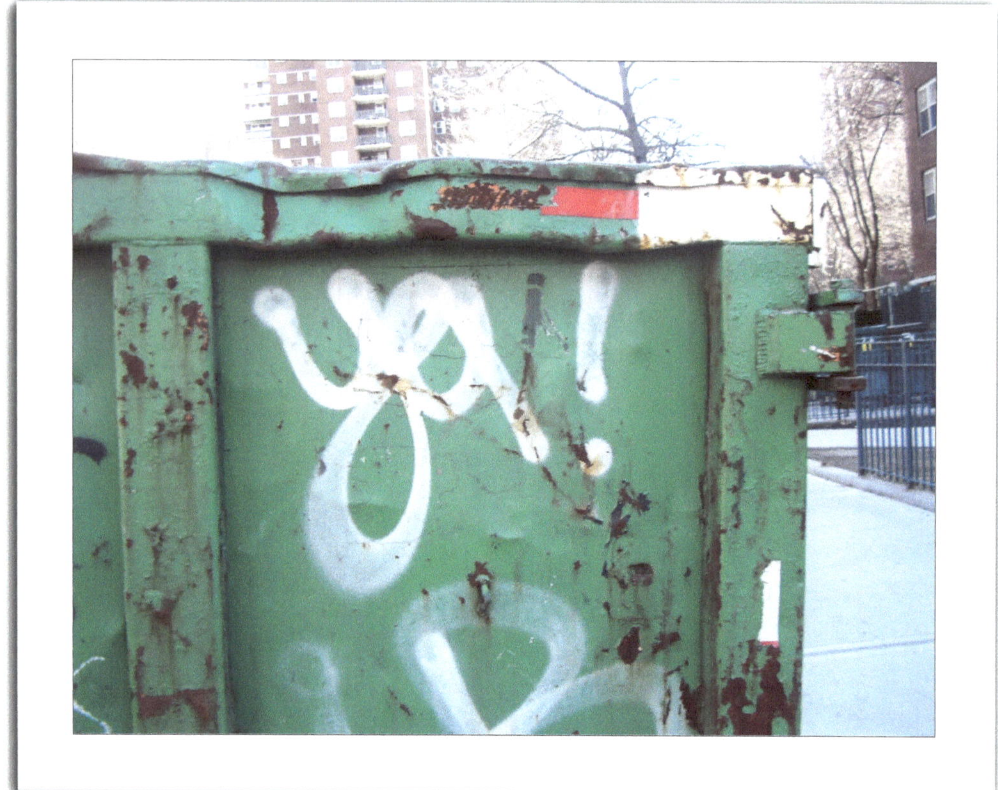

Original Tag

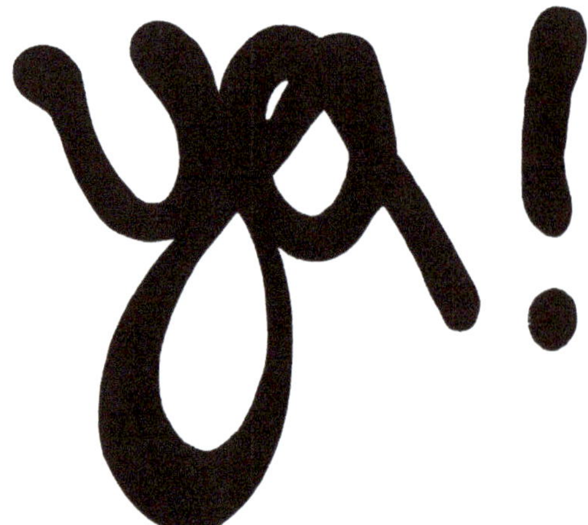

My Copy

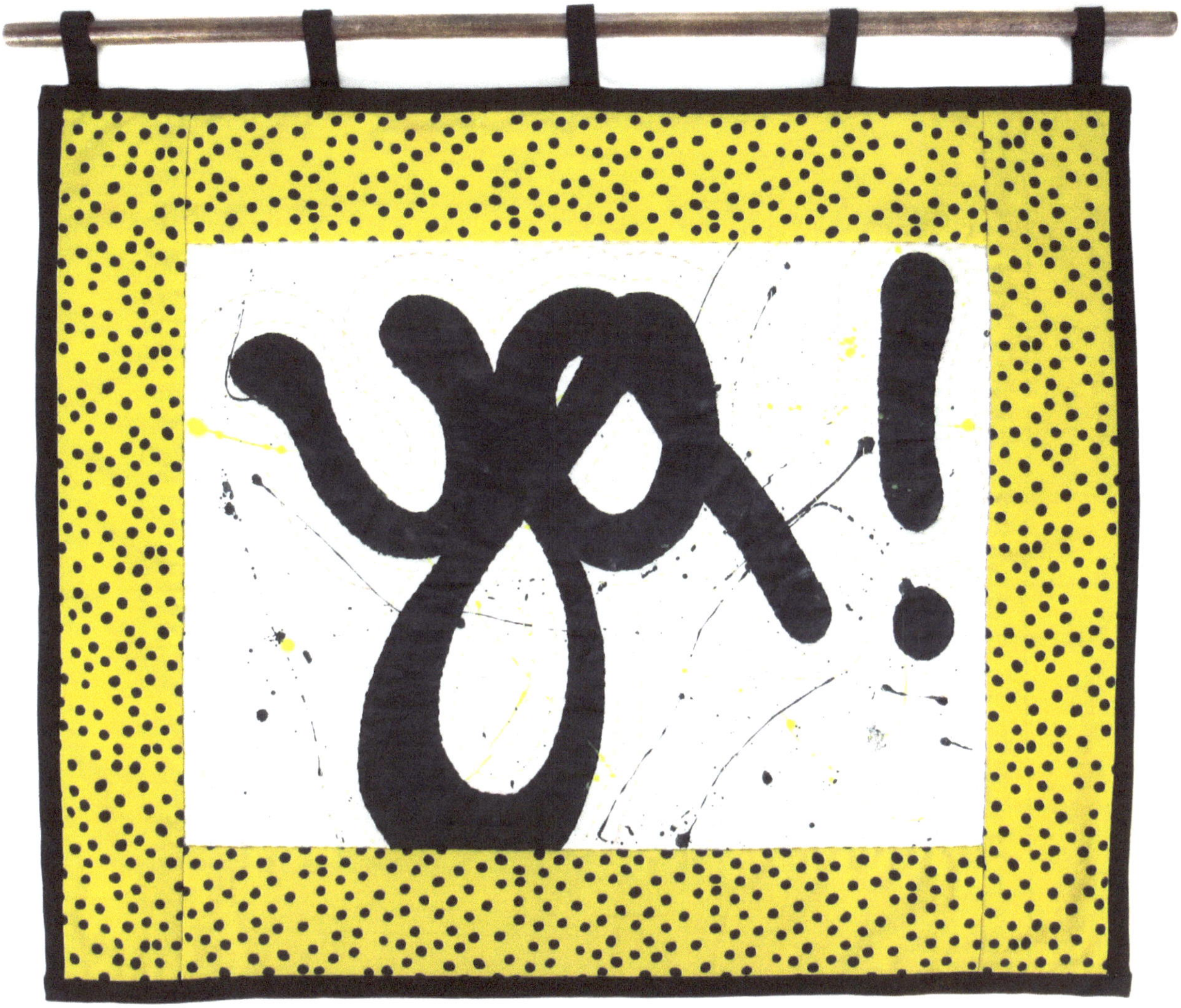

Quilt Front

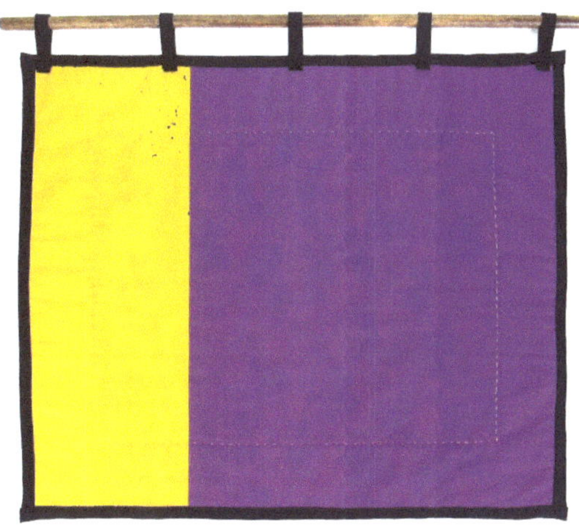

Quilt Back

Finished Quilt Size: 17" x 21"
Border: 3"
Binding: Double-Fold, Extra-Wide Bias Tape
Back: 17" x 21" Scrap Fabric

SKATE

Skate Park - Santa Rosa, California

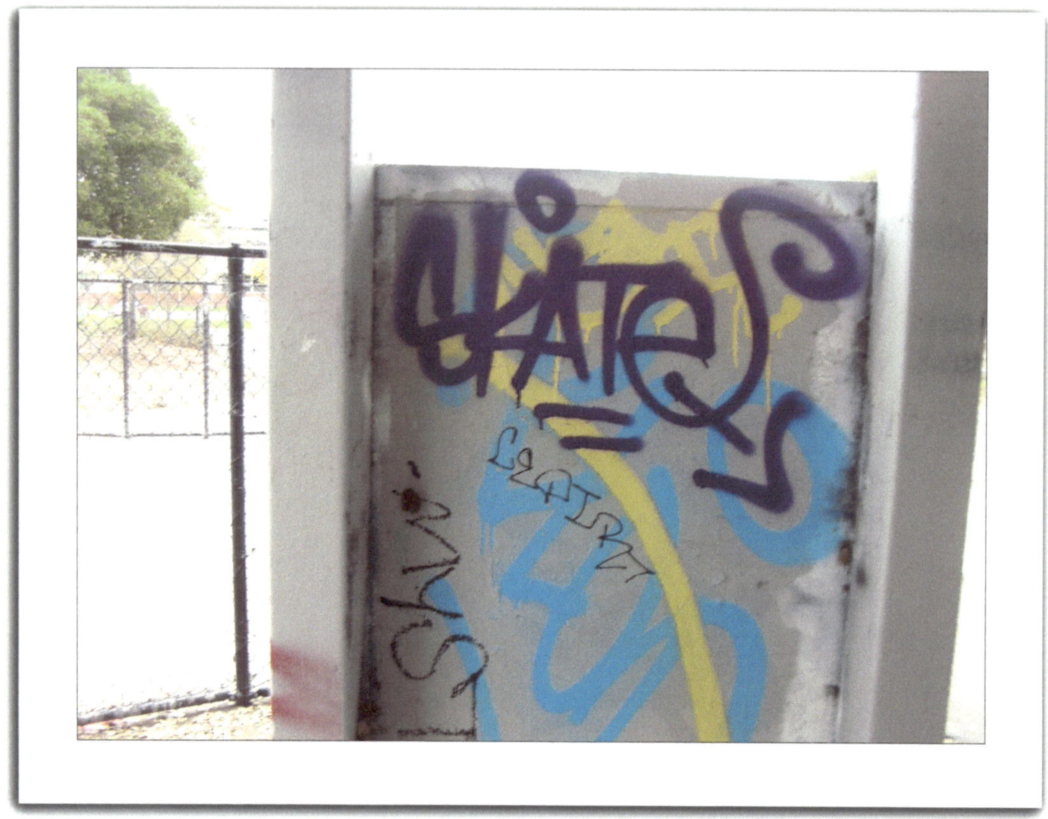

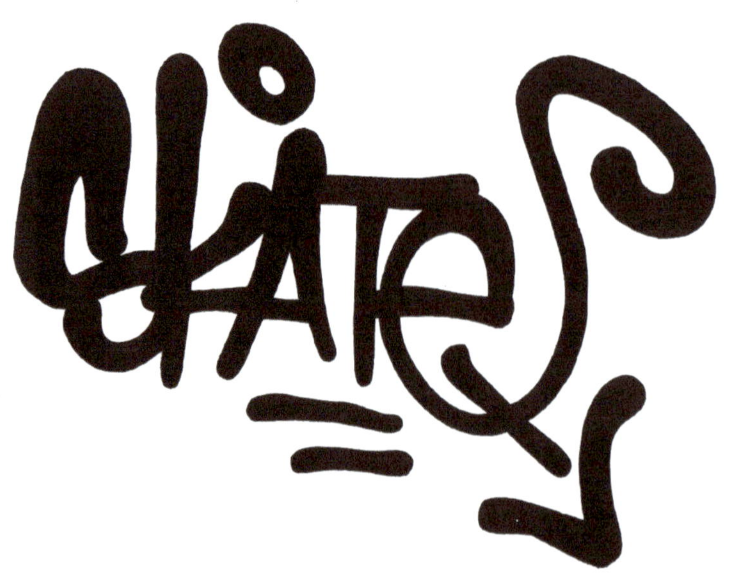

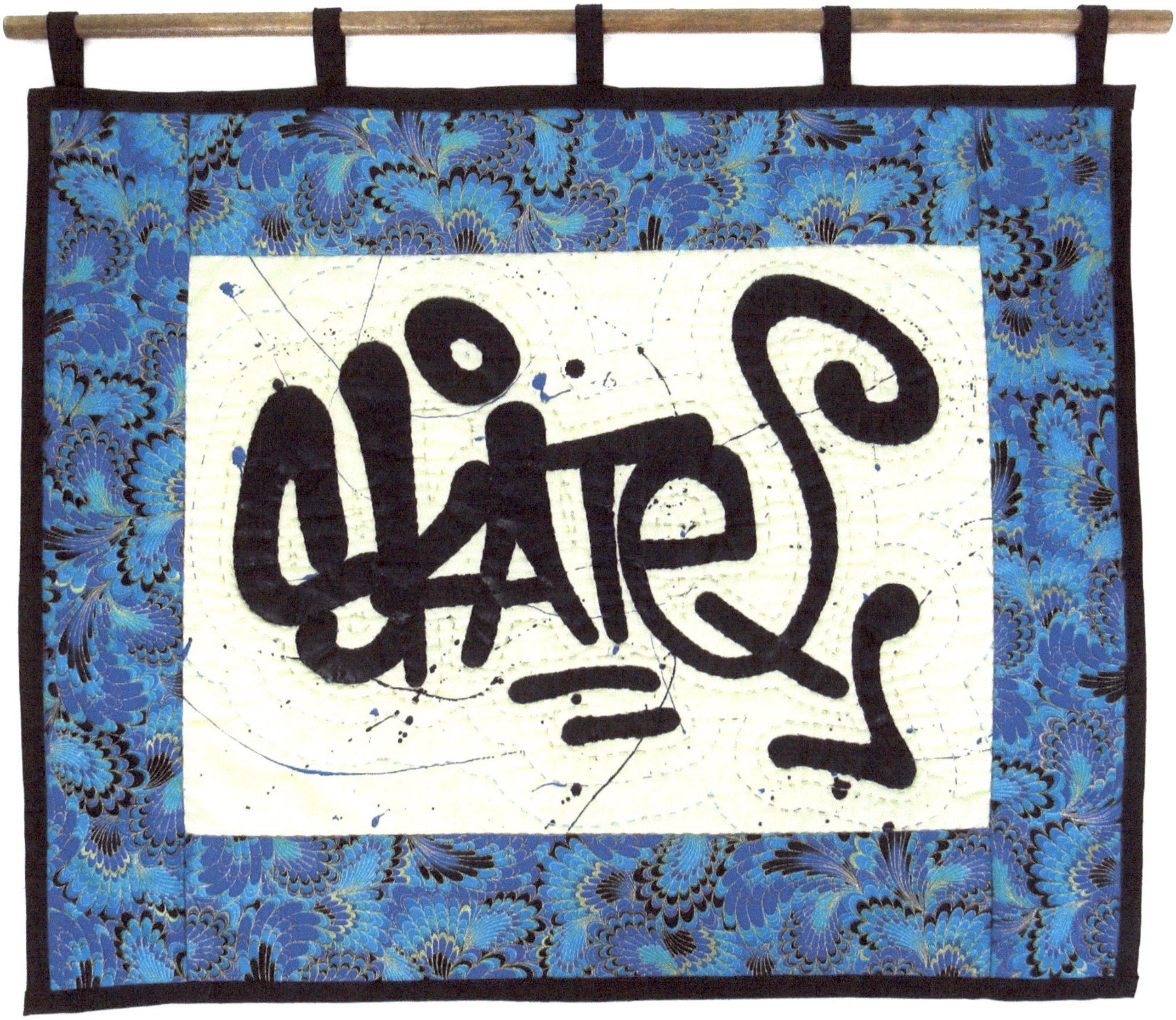

Finished Quilt Size: 17 1/2" x 21 1/2"
Border: 3"
Binding: Double-Fold, Extra-Wide Bias Tape
Back: 17 1/2" x 21 1/2" Scrap Fabric

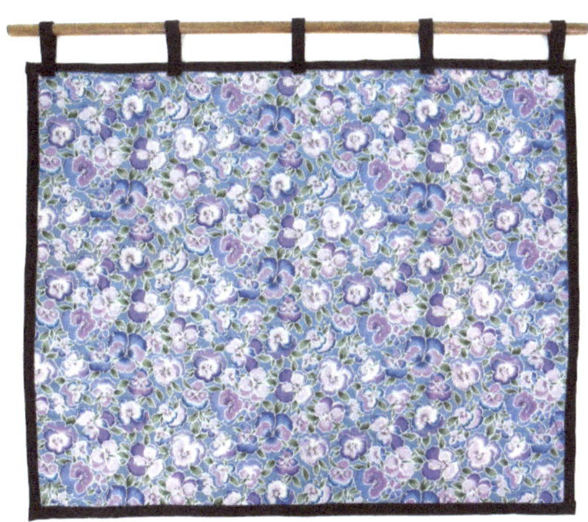

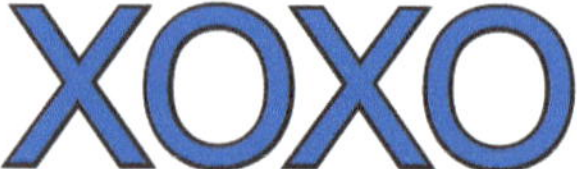

Roll-down Gate - Manhattan, New York City

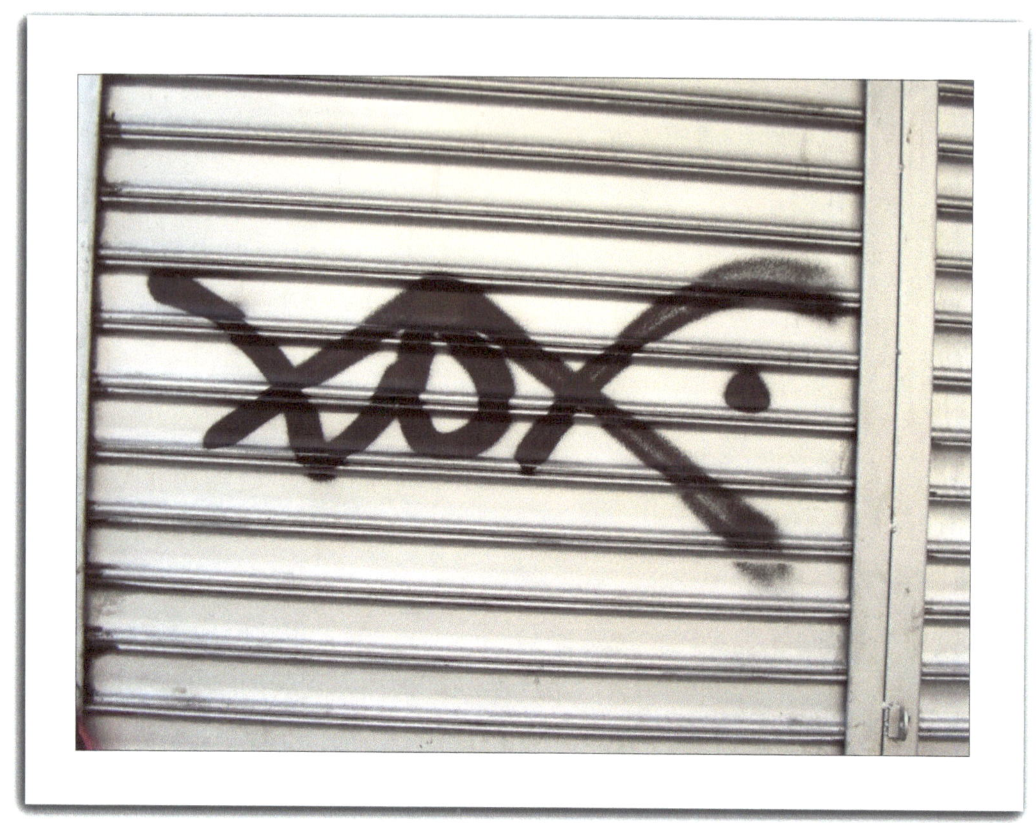

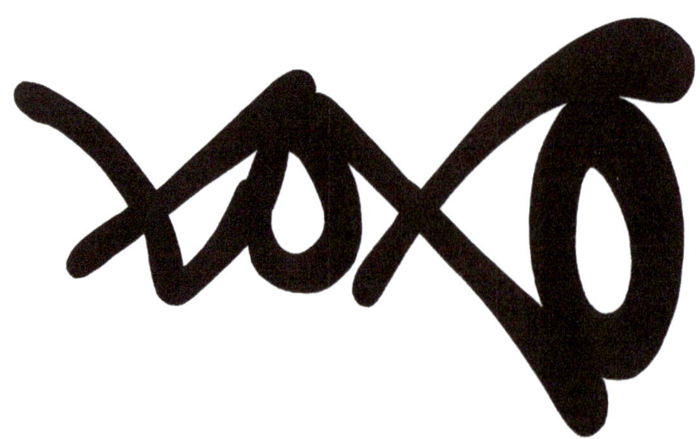

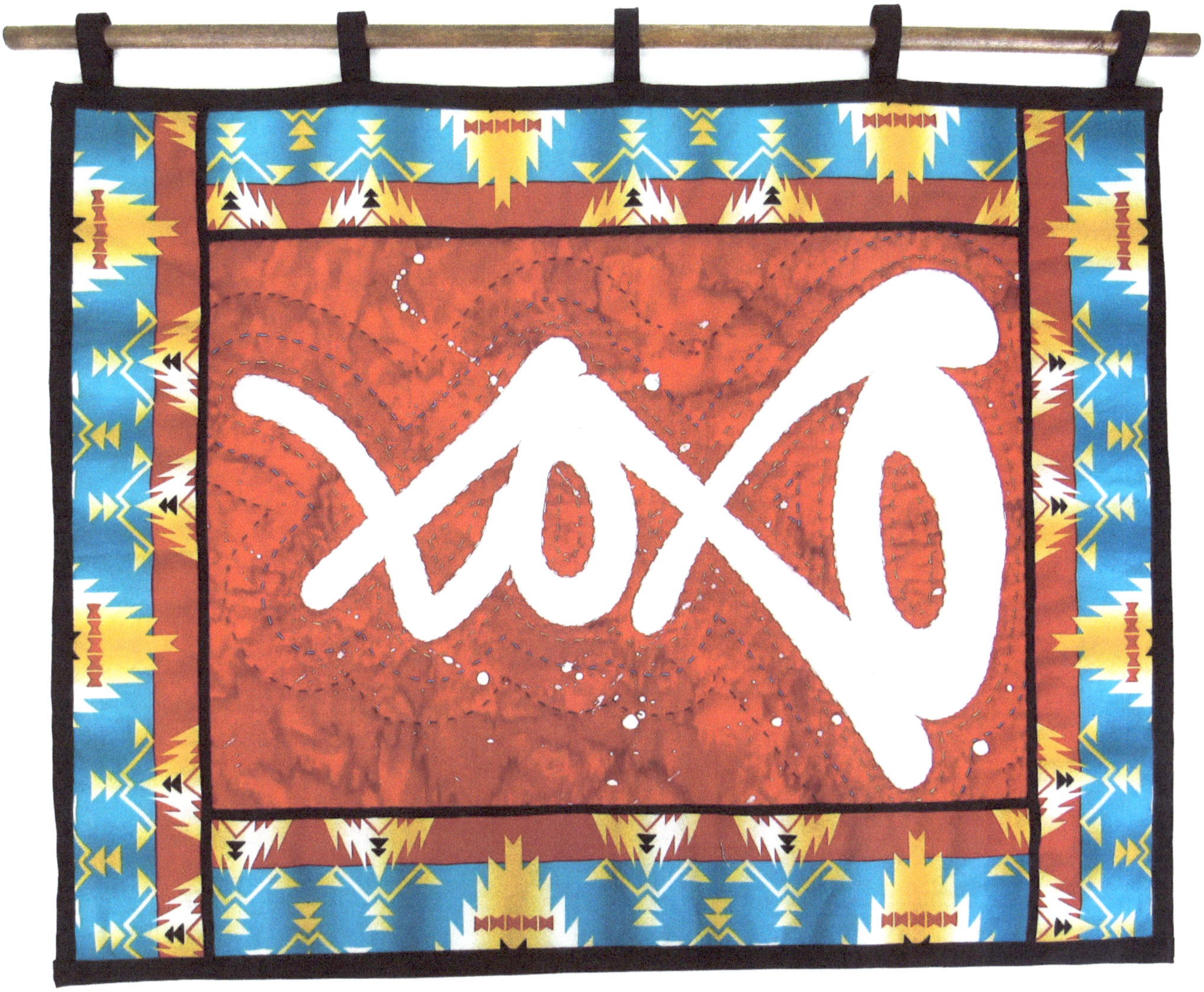

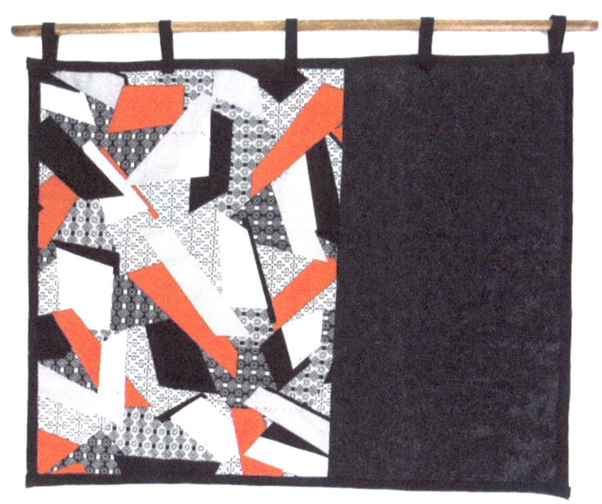

Finished Quilt Size: 17” x 22 1/2”
Border: 3”
Binding: Double-Fold, Extra-Wide Bias Tape
Back: 17” x 22 1/2” Scrap Fabric

KURE

Dumpster - Santa Rosa, California

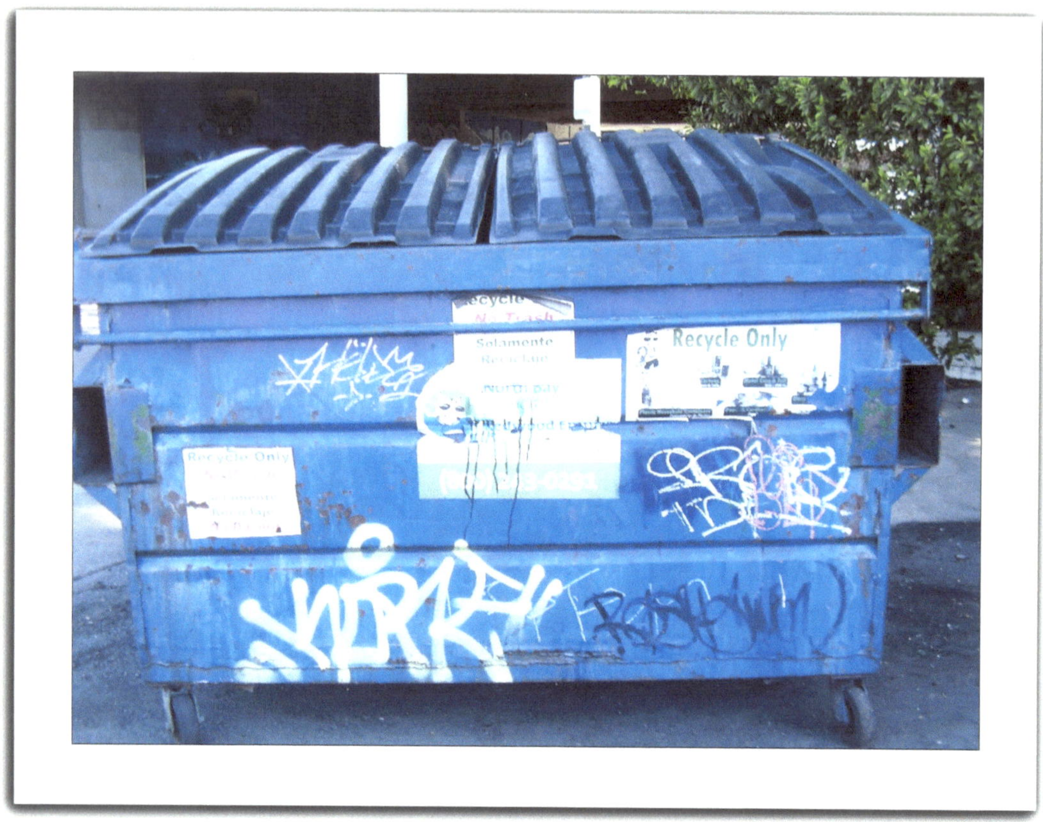

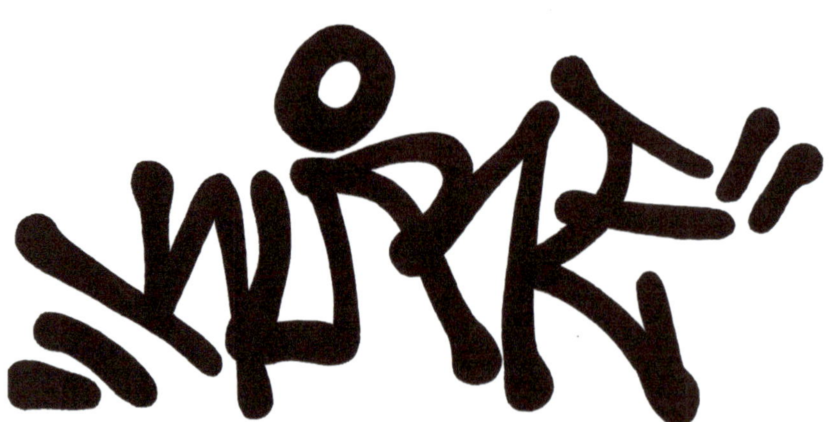

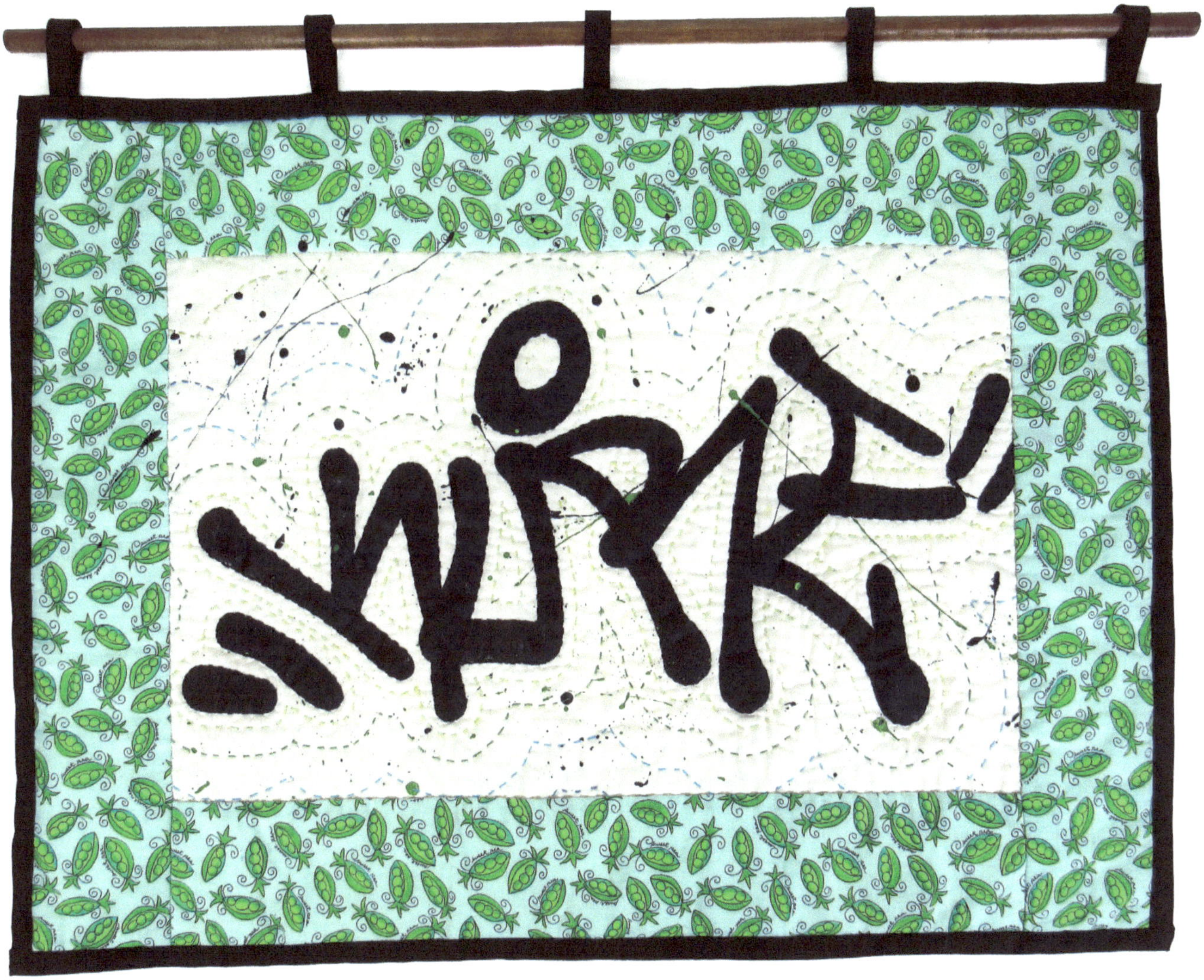

Finished Quilt Size: 16 1/2" x 22 1/2"
Border: 3"
Binding: Double-Fold, Extra-Wide Bias Tape
Back: 16 1/2" x 22 1/2" Scrap Fabric

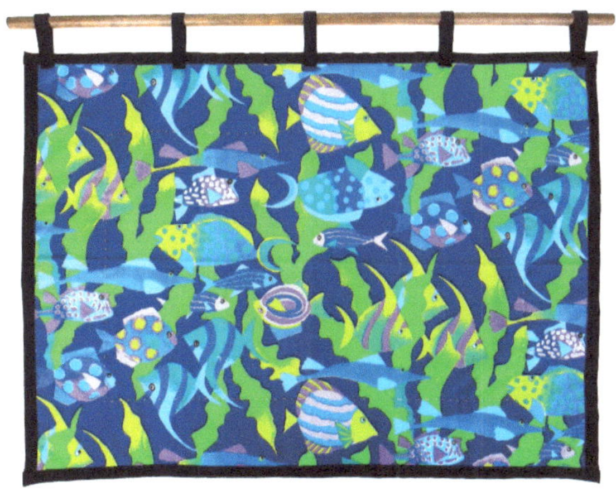

QWILTS.

Dumpster - Portland, Oregon

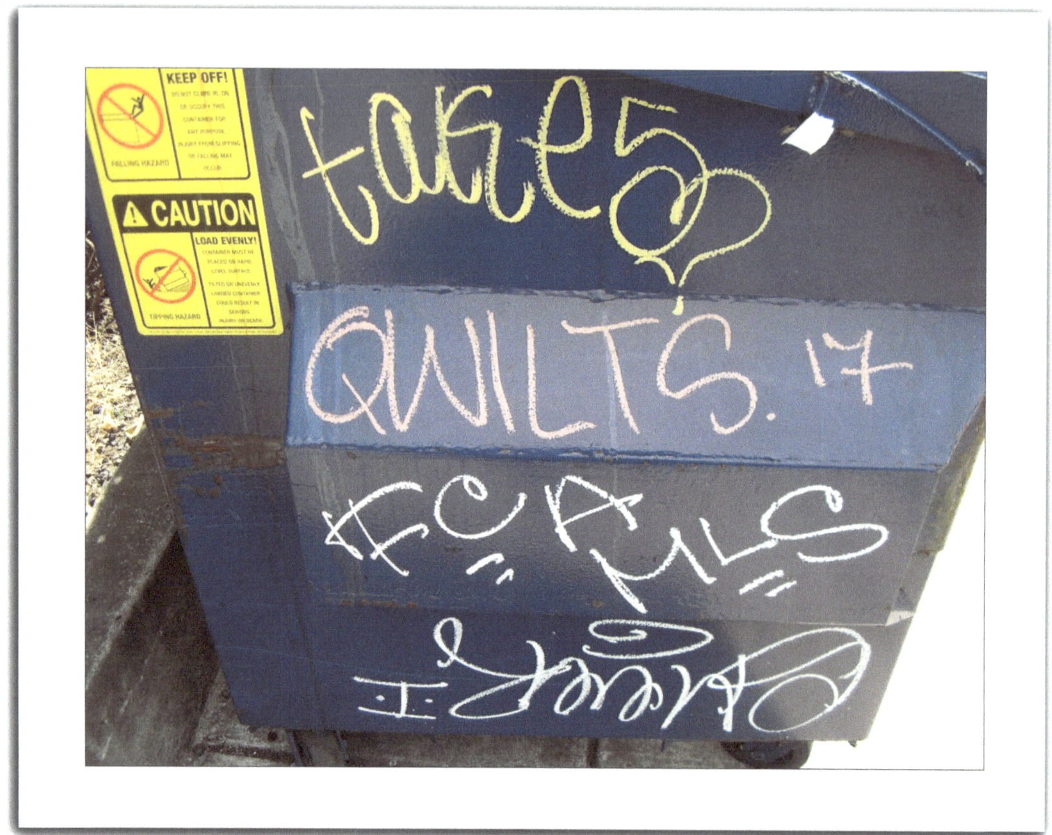

QWILTS.

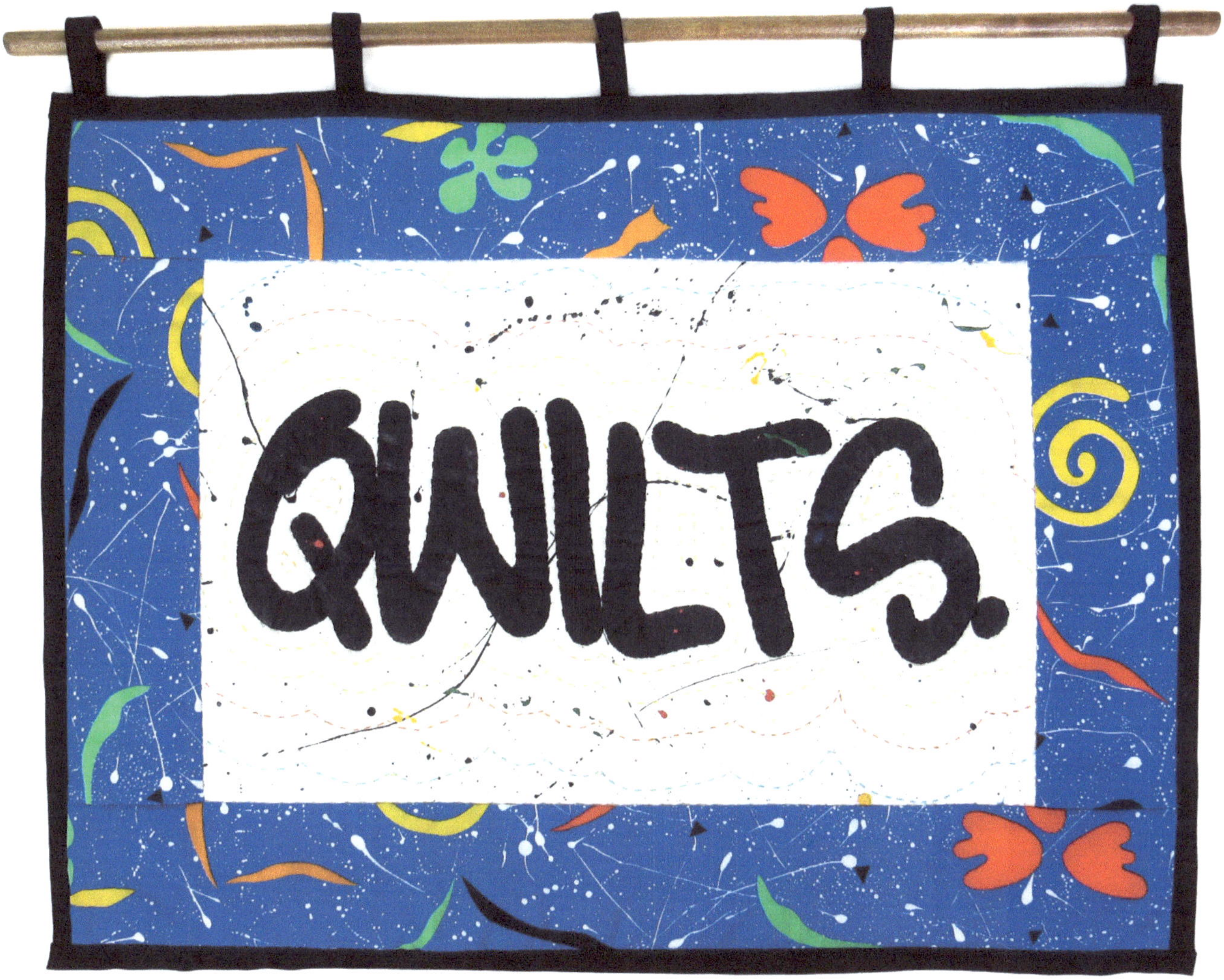

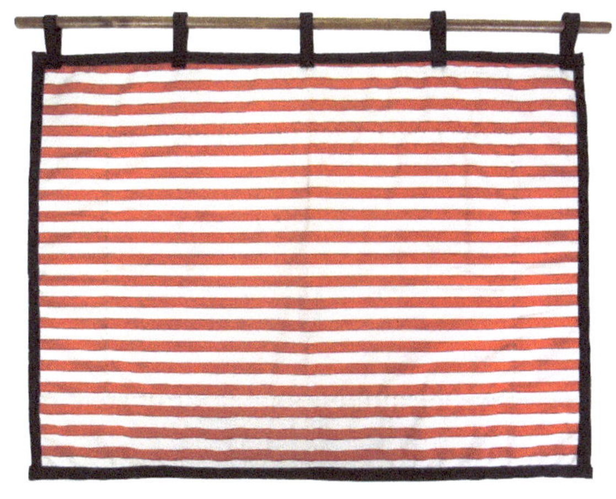

Finished Quilt Size: 16” x 22 1/2”
Border: 3”
Binding: Double-Fold, Extra-Wide Bias Tape
Back: 16” x 22 1/2” Scrap Fabric

SUNSHINE

Bridge Support - Somewhere in Washington State

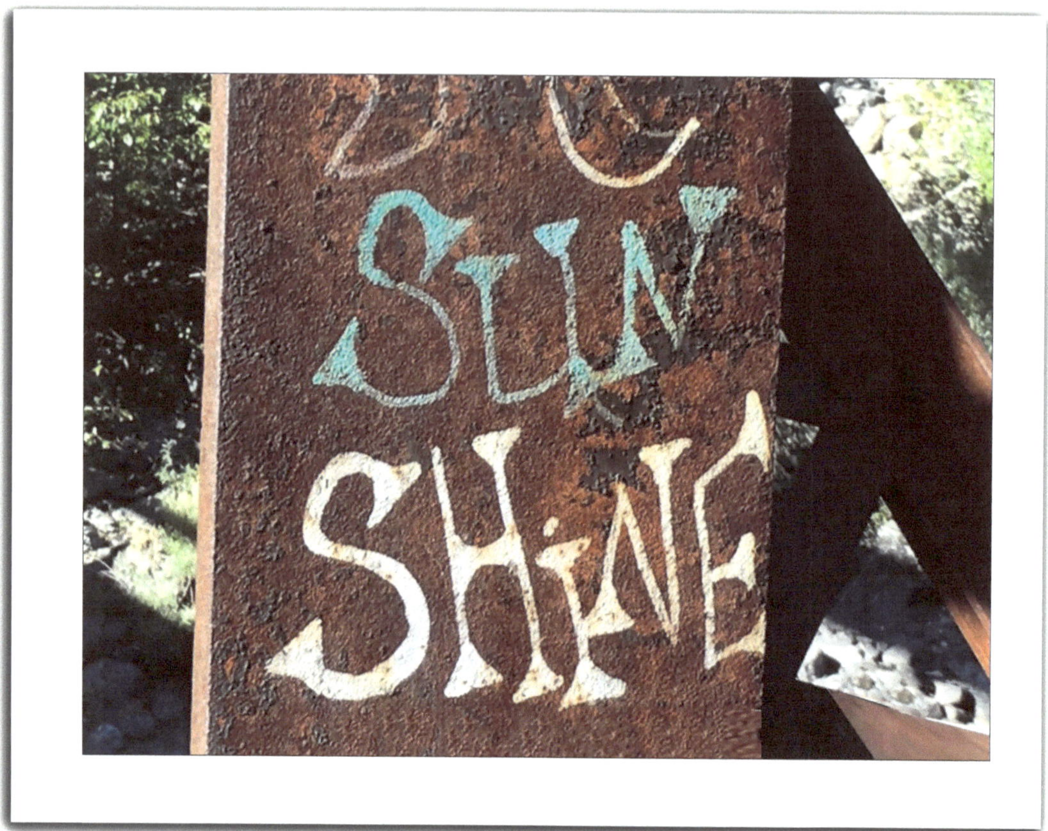

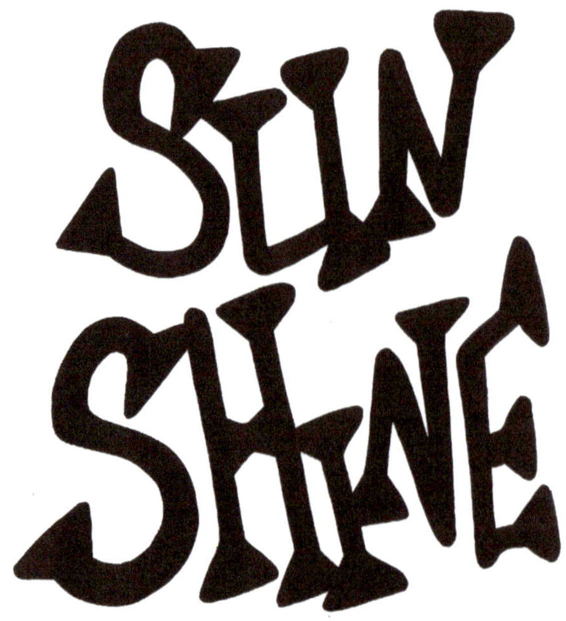

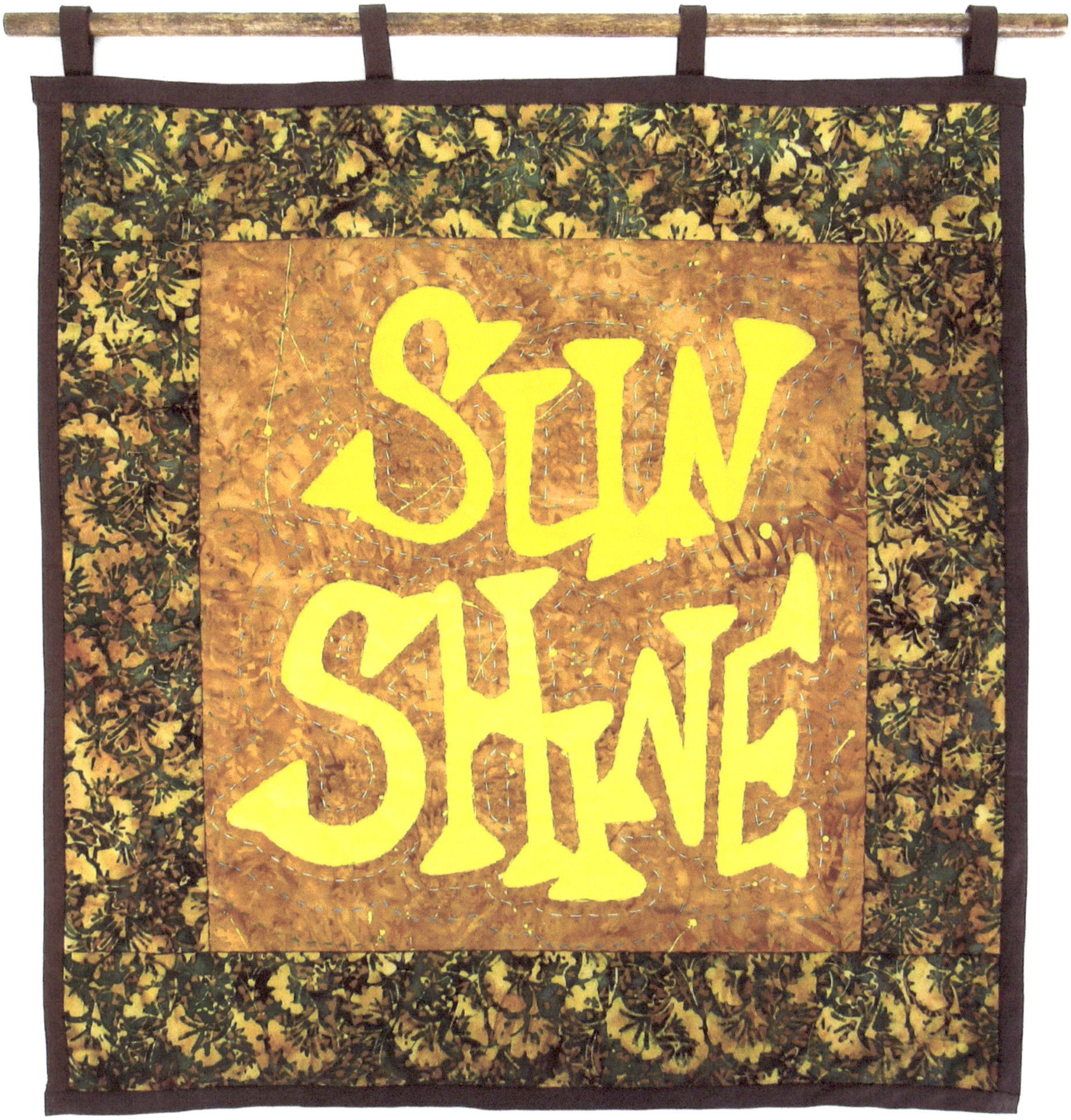

NOTE: I forgot to dot the 'i'.

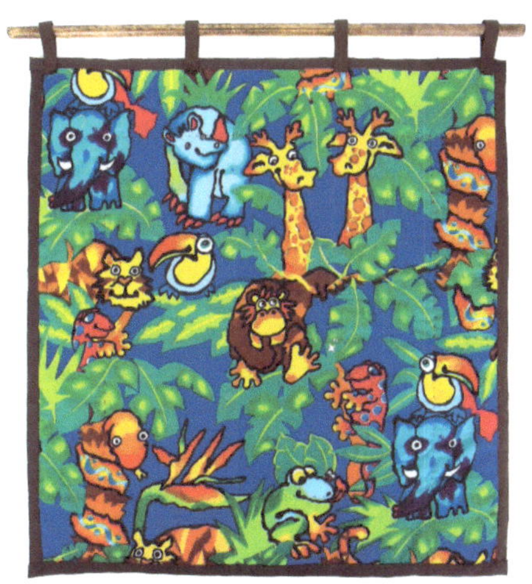

Finished Quilt Size: 19 1/2" x 19"
Border: 3"
Binding: Double-Fold, Extra-Wide Bias Tape
Back: 19 1/2" x 19" Scrap Fabric

NEVR

I can't place this tag - Somewhere in New York City

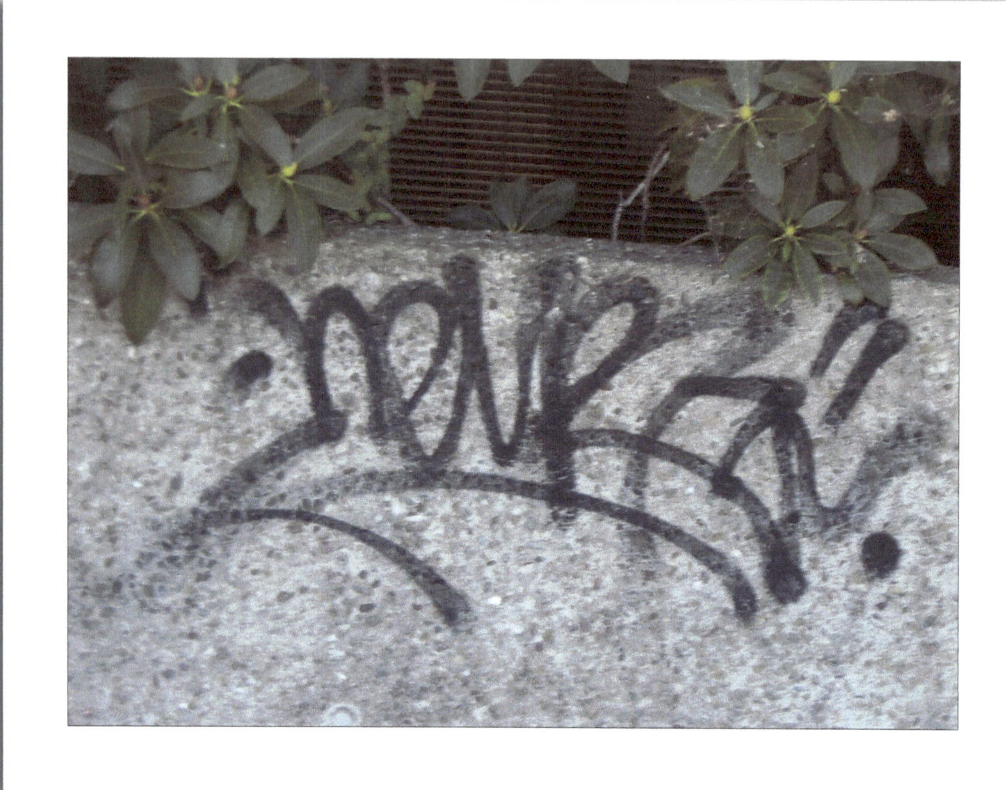

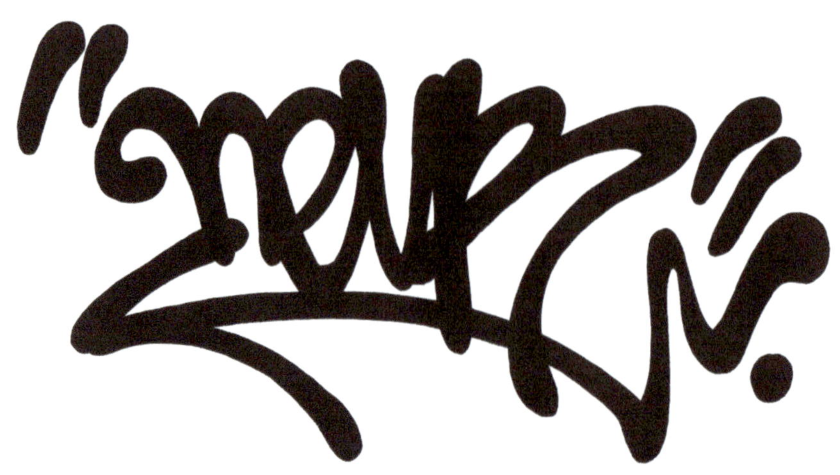

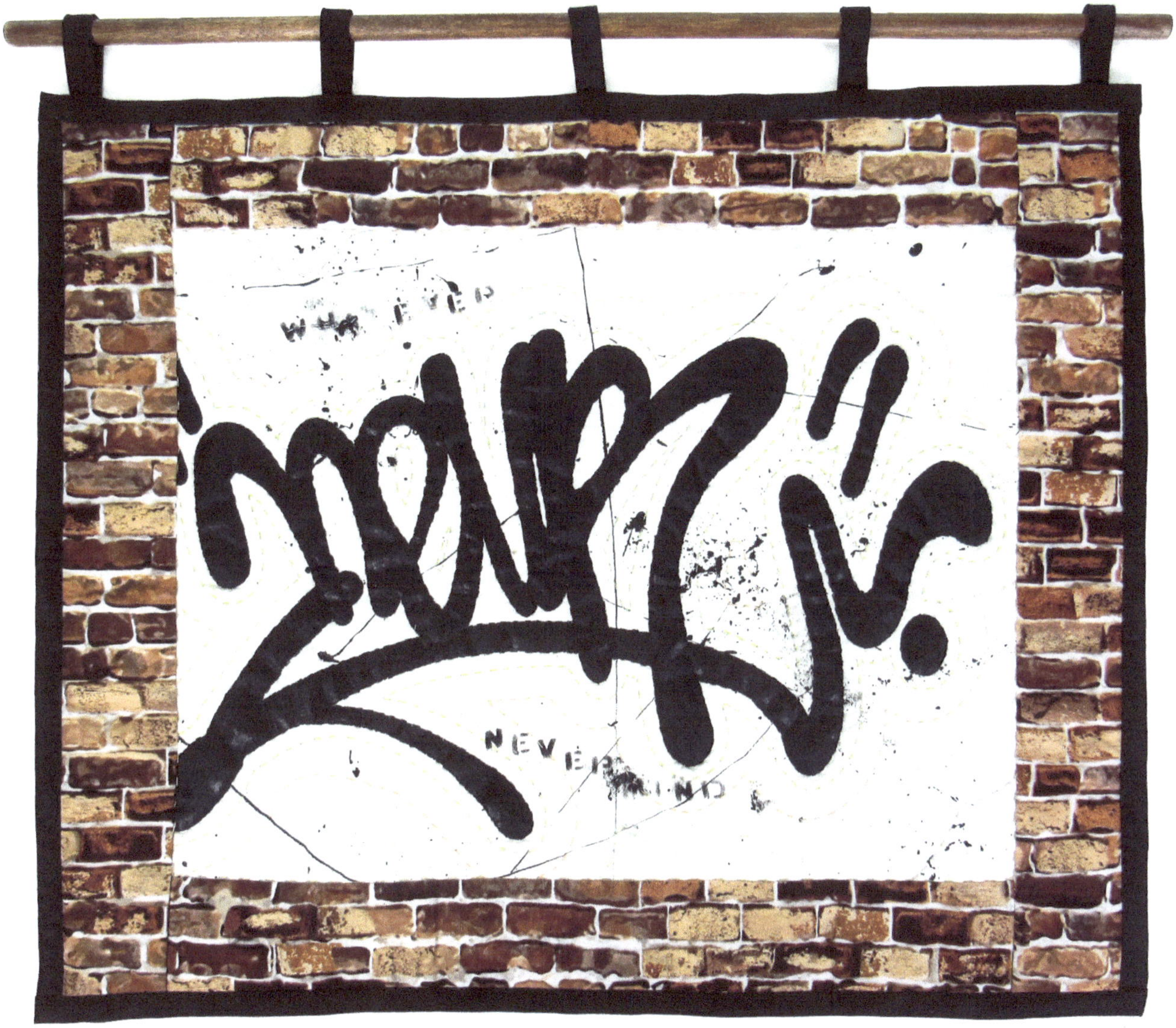

NOTE: The original tag reads NEVR 1.

Finished Quilt Size: 17” x 20 1/2”
Border: 2 1/2”
Binding: Double-Fold, Extra-Wide Bias Tape
Back: 17” x 20 1/2” Scrap Fabric

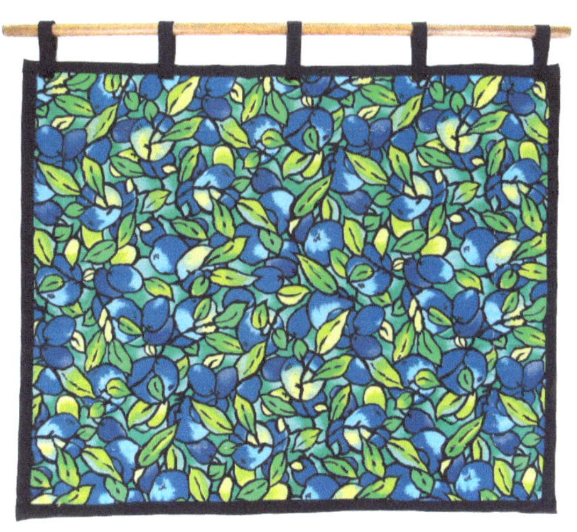

HURT

Sheet Metal Fence - Brooklyn, New York City

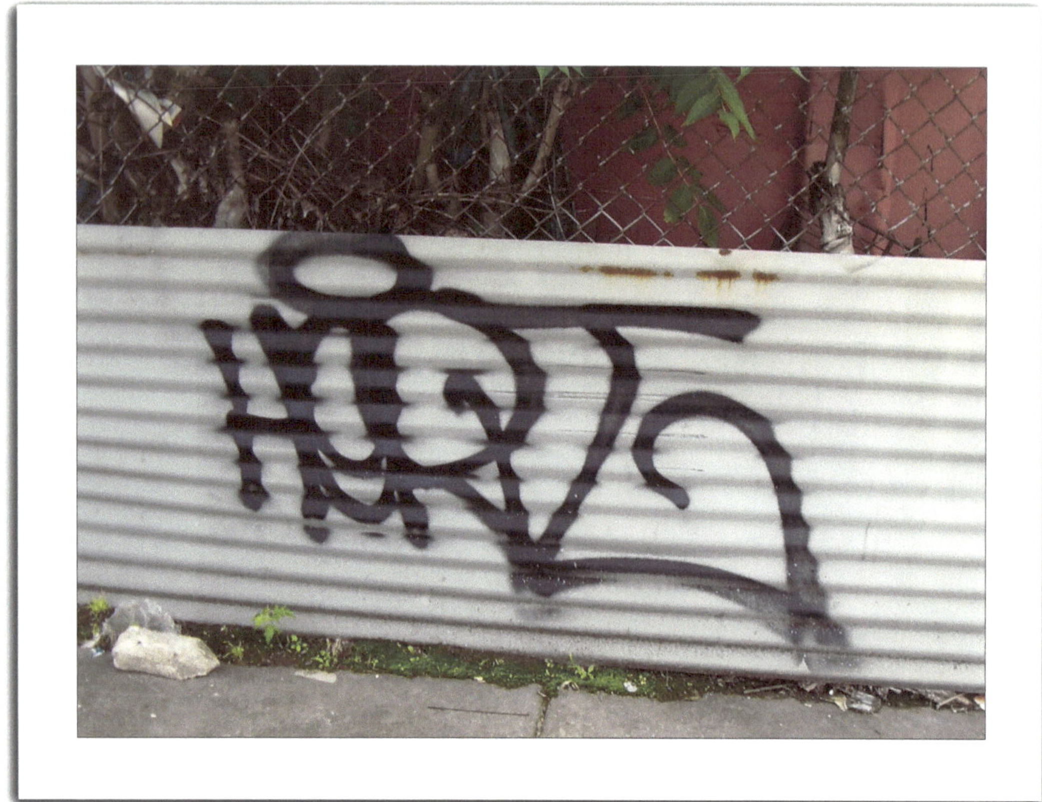

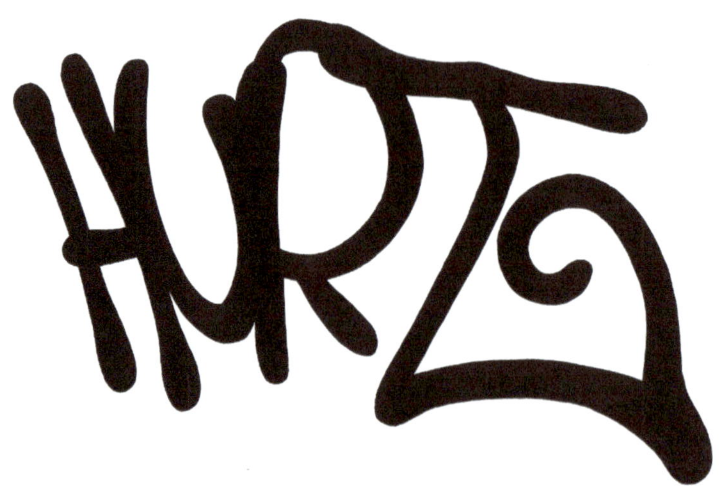

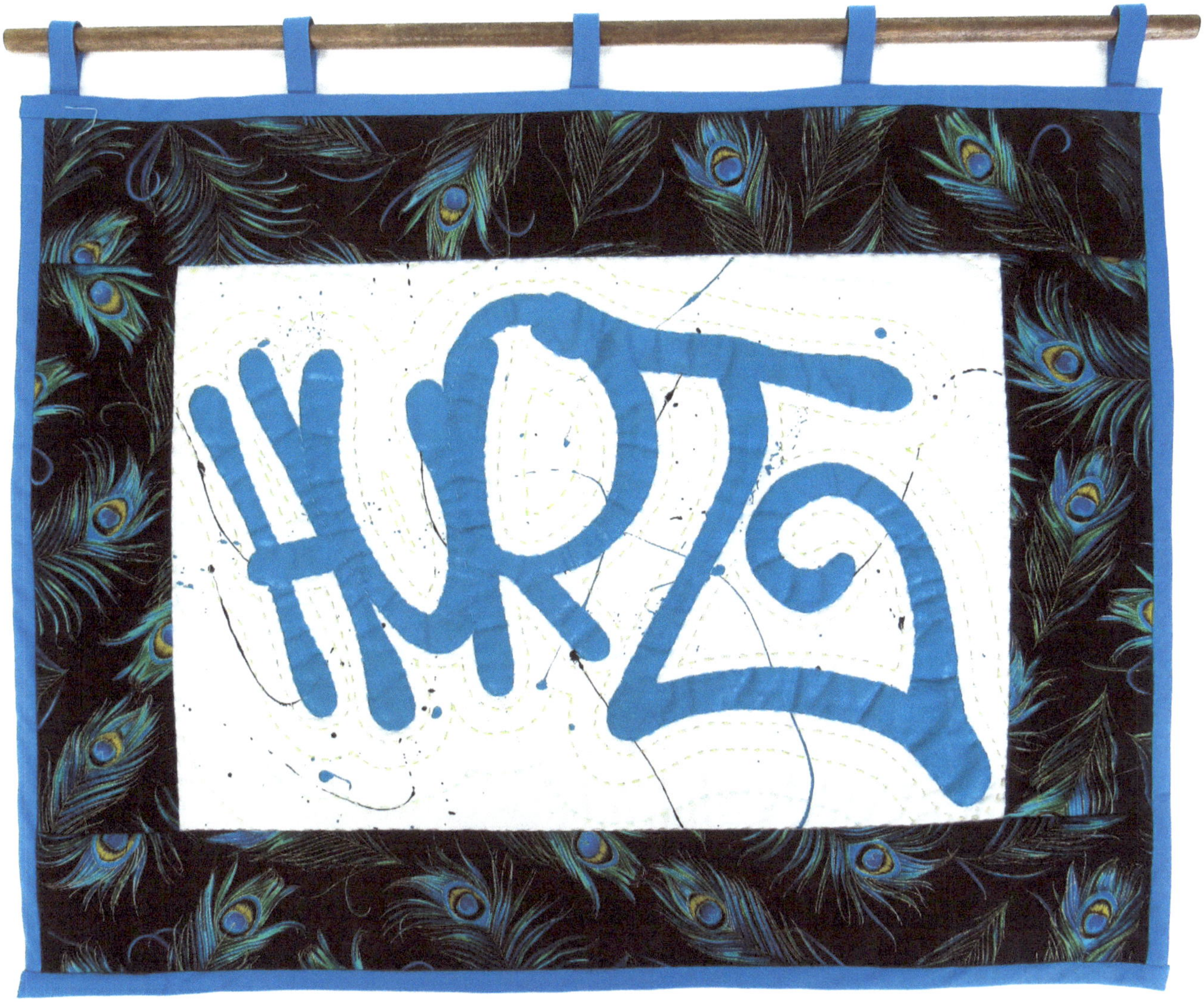

NOTE: I changed this tag from HERT to HURT. In retrospect I should have kept the 'E'.

Finished Quilt Size: 6 1/2" x 21 1/2"
Border: 3"
Binding: Double-Fold, Extra-Wide Bias Tape
Back: 6 1/2" x 21 1/2" Scrap Fabric

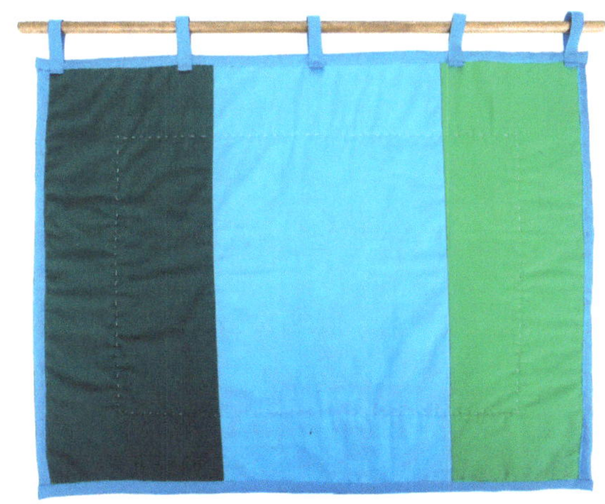

SICK

Apartment Door - DUMBO, New York City

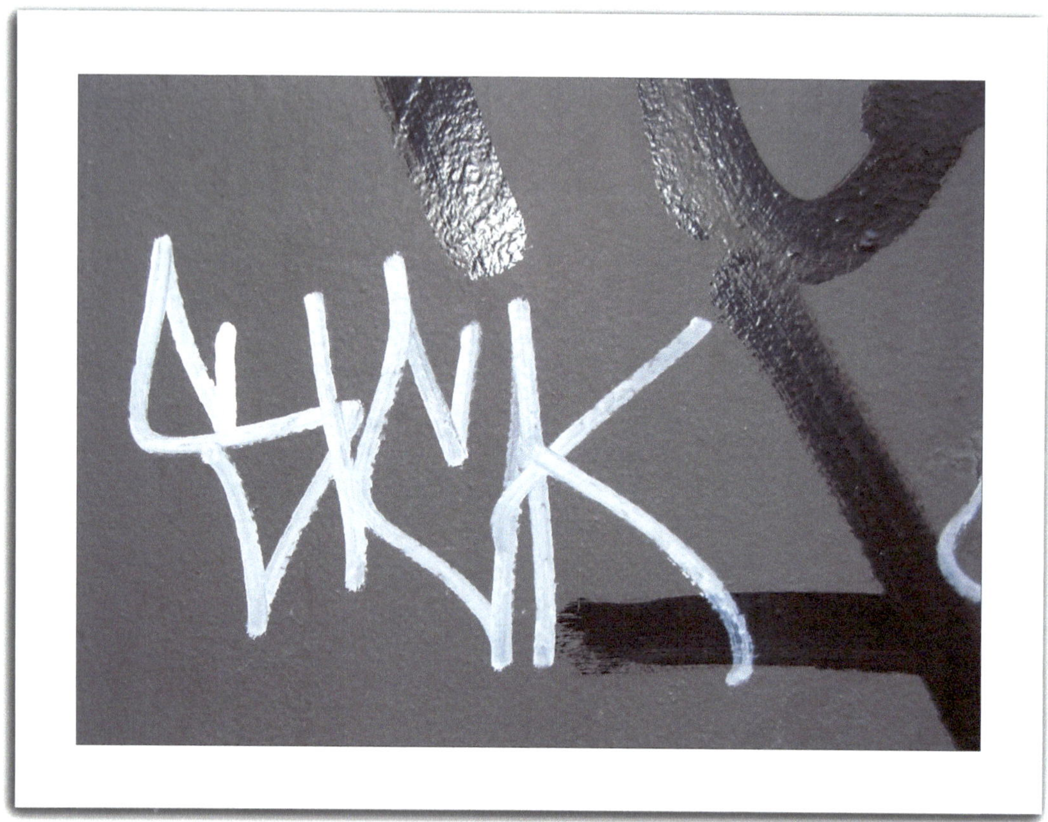

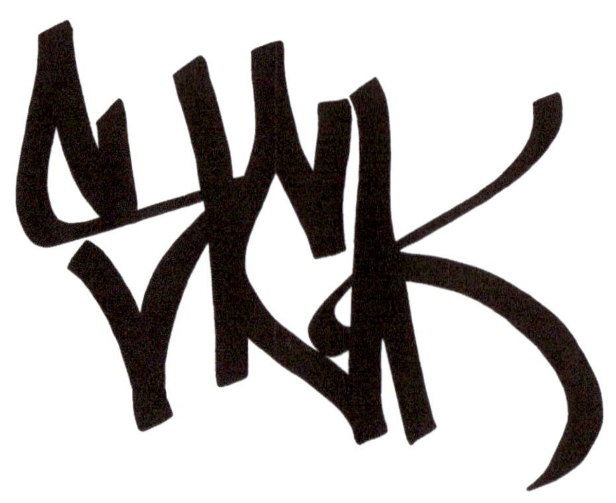

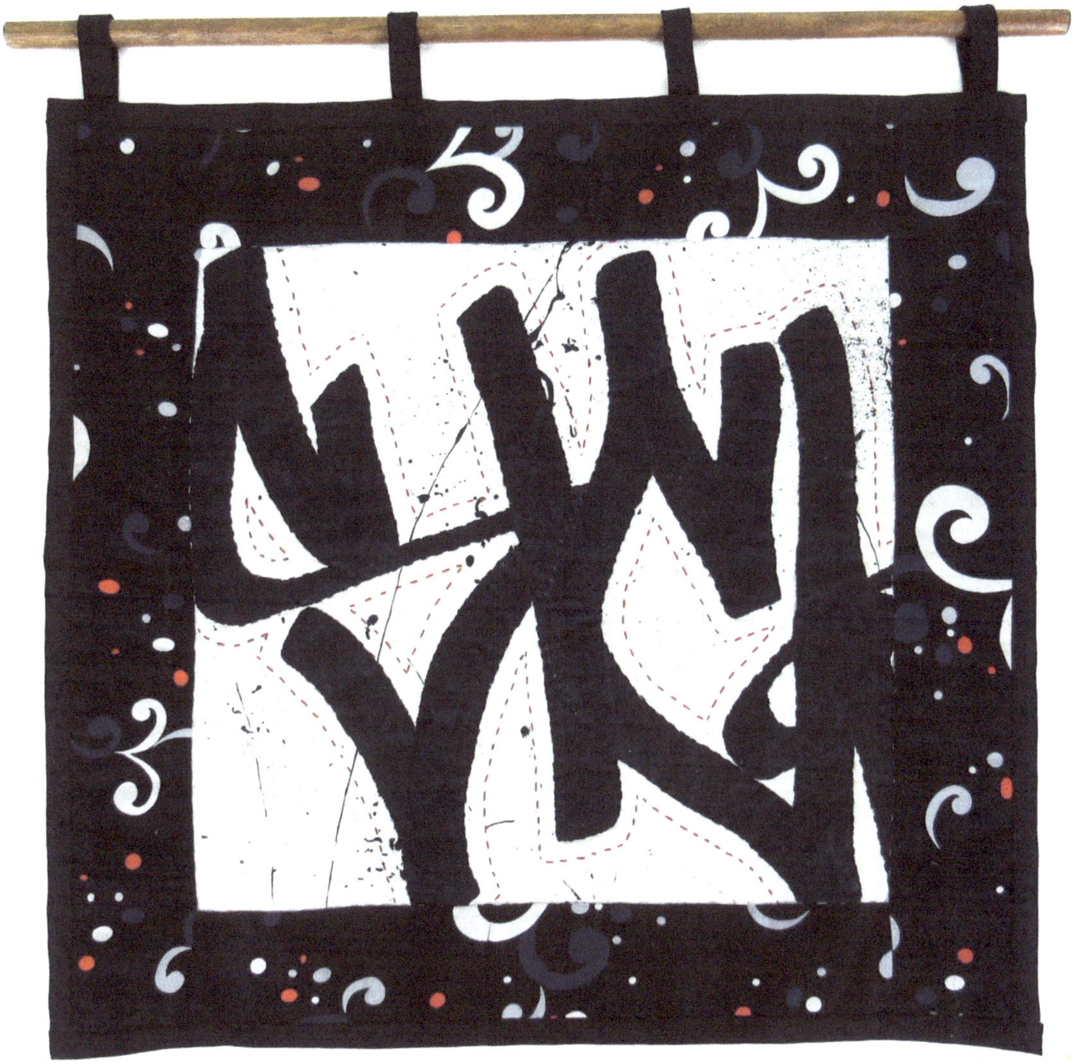

NOTE: I tried cropping this tag to make it more dramatic. Did it work?

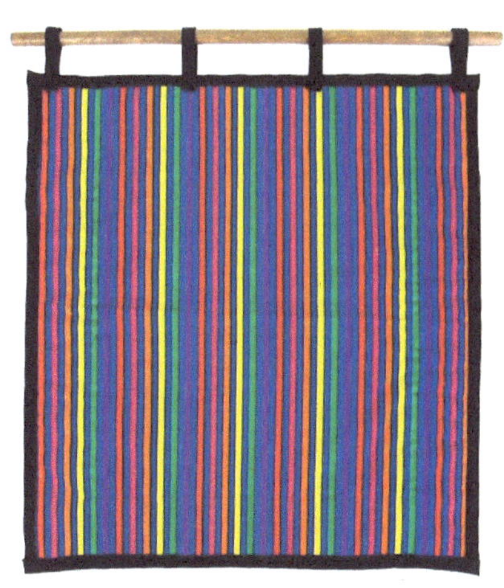

Finished Quilt Size: 16" x 16"
Border: 2 1/2"
Binding: Double-Fold, Extra-Wide Bias Tape
Back: 16" x 16" Scrap Fabric

NERVE

Delivery Truck - Bensonhurst, New York City

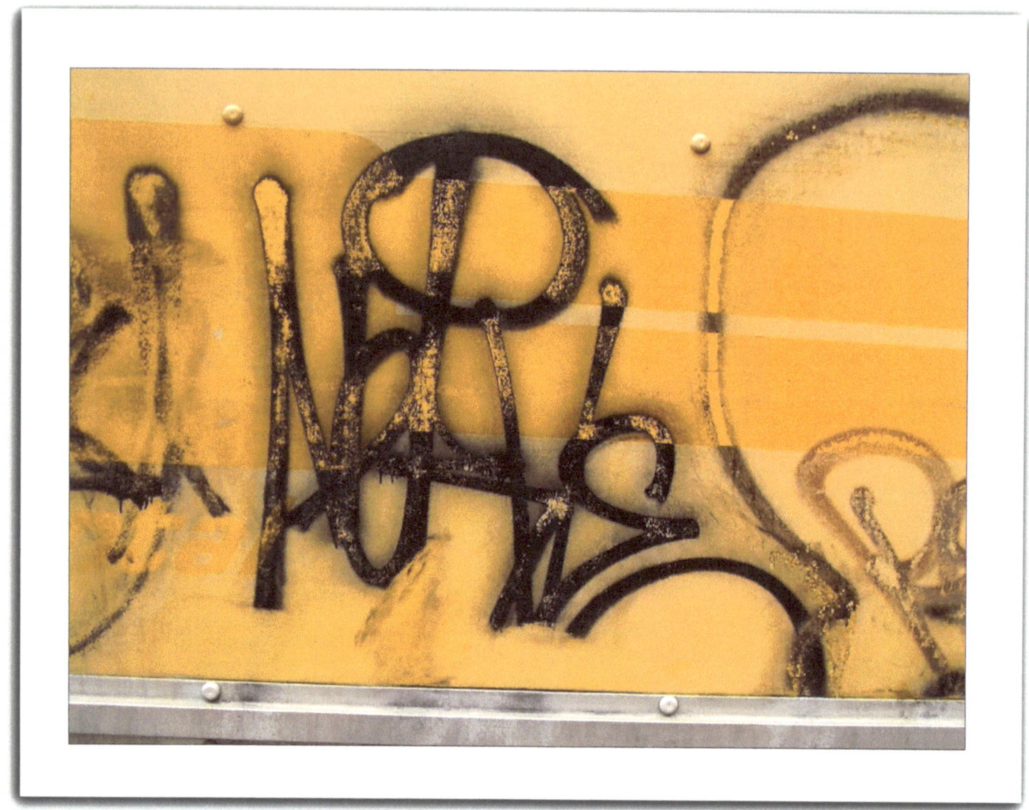

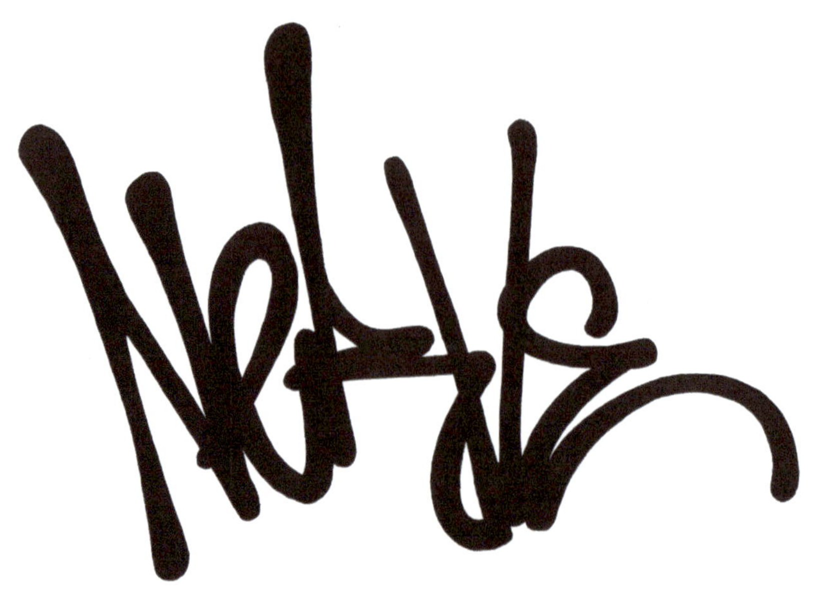

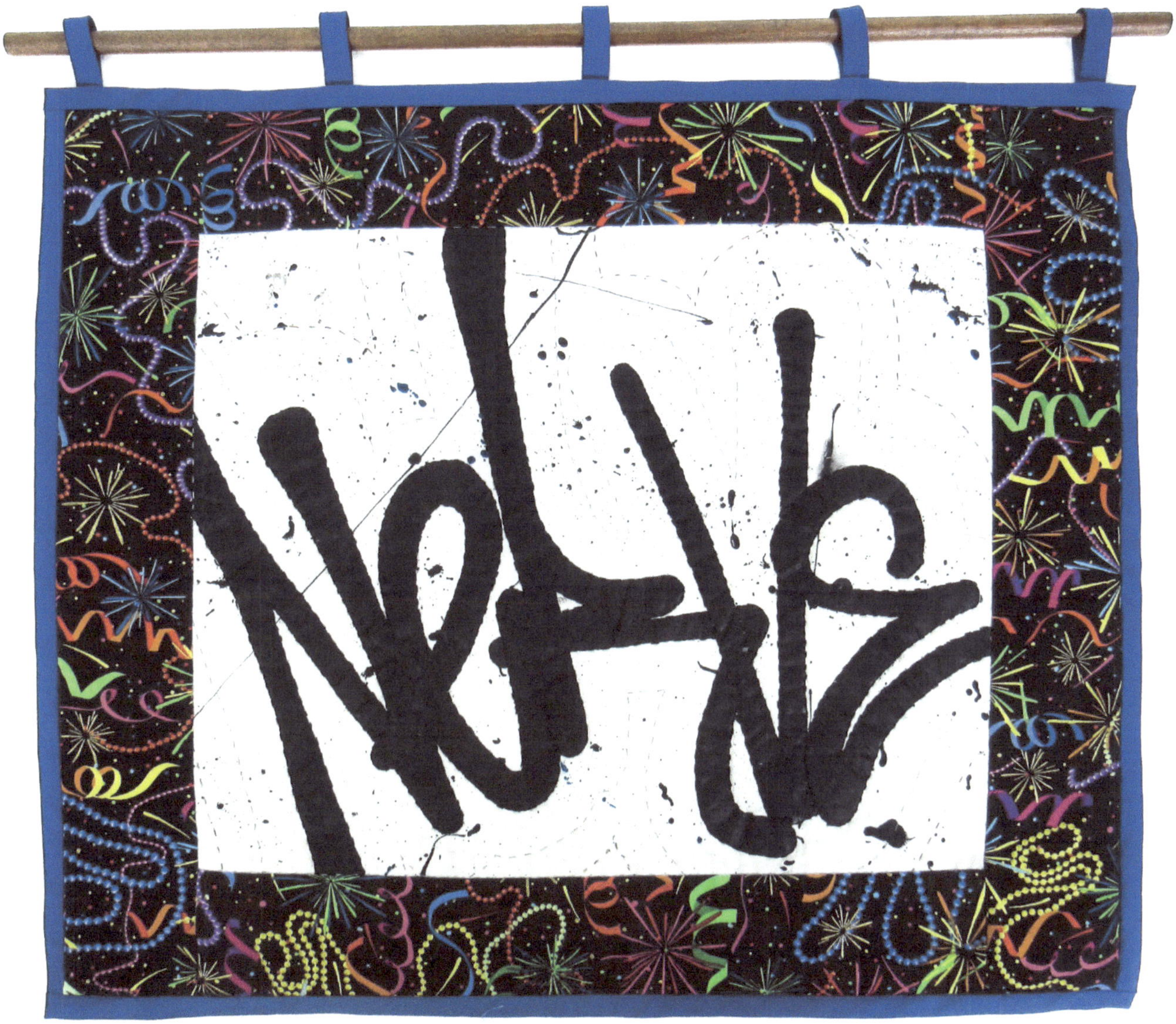

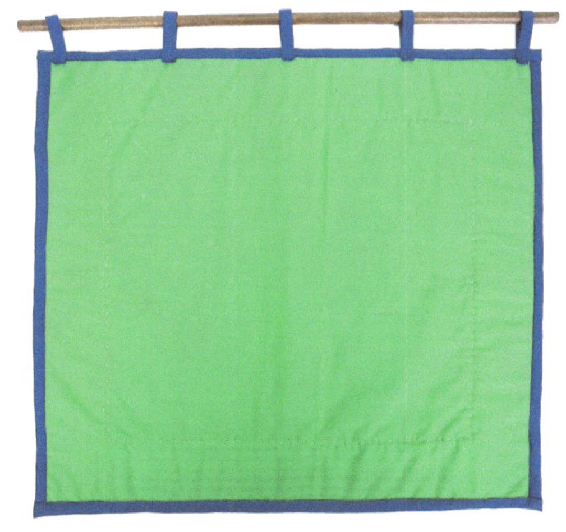

Finished Quilt Size: 18 1/2" x 21"
Border: 3"
Binding: Double-Fold, Extra-Wide Bias Tape
Back: 18 1/2" x 21" Scrap Fabric

DUDE

Delivery Truck - Sunset Park, New York City

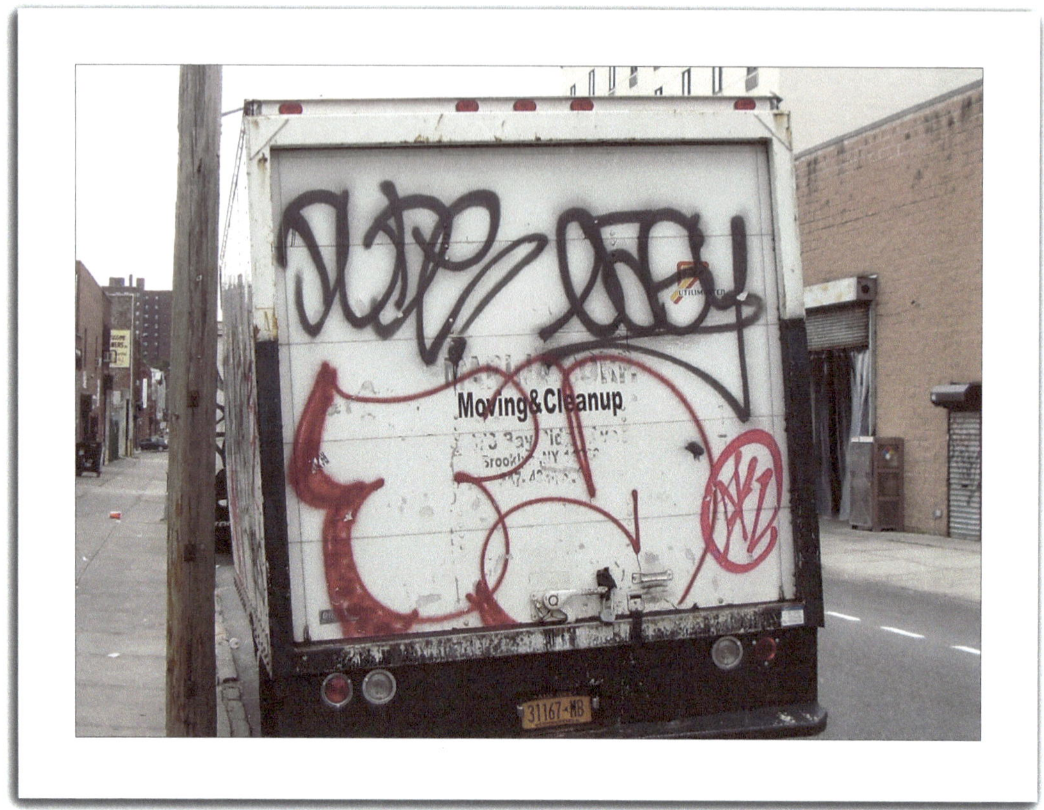

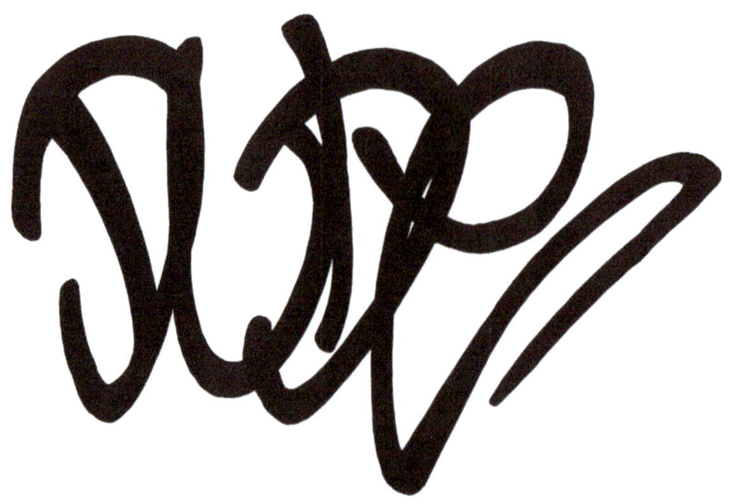

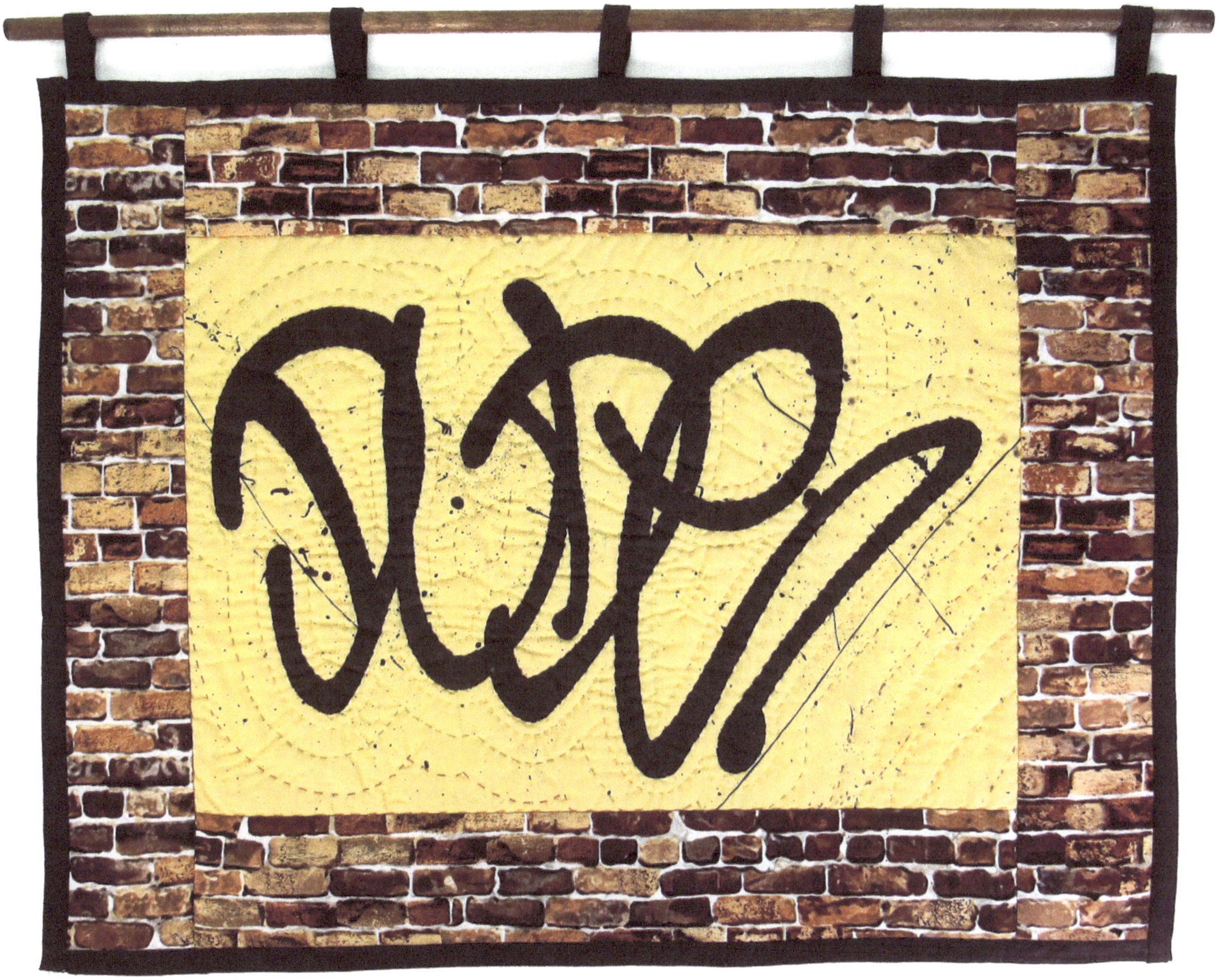

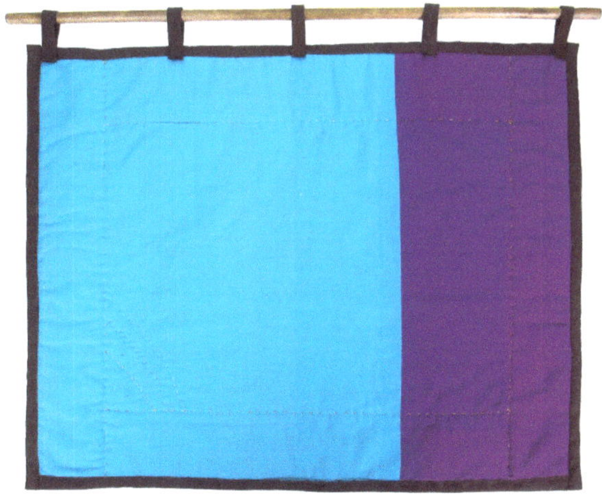

Finished Quilt Size: 17" x 22 1/2"
Border: 3"
Binding: Double-Fold, Extra-Wide Bias Tape
Back: 17" x 22 1/2" Scrap Fabric

MYTH

Train Tracks - Brooklyn, New York City

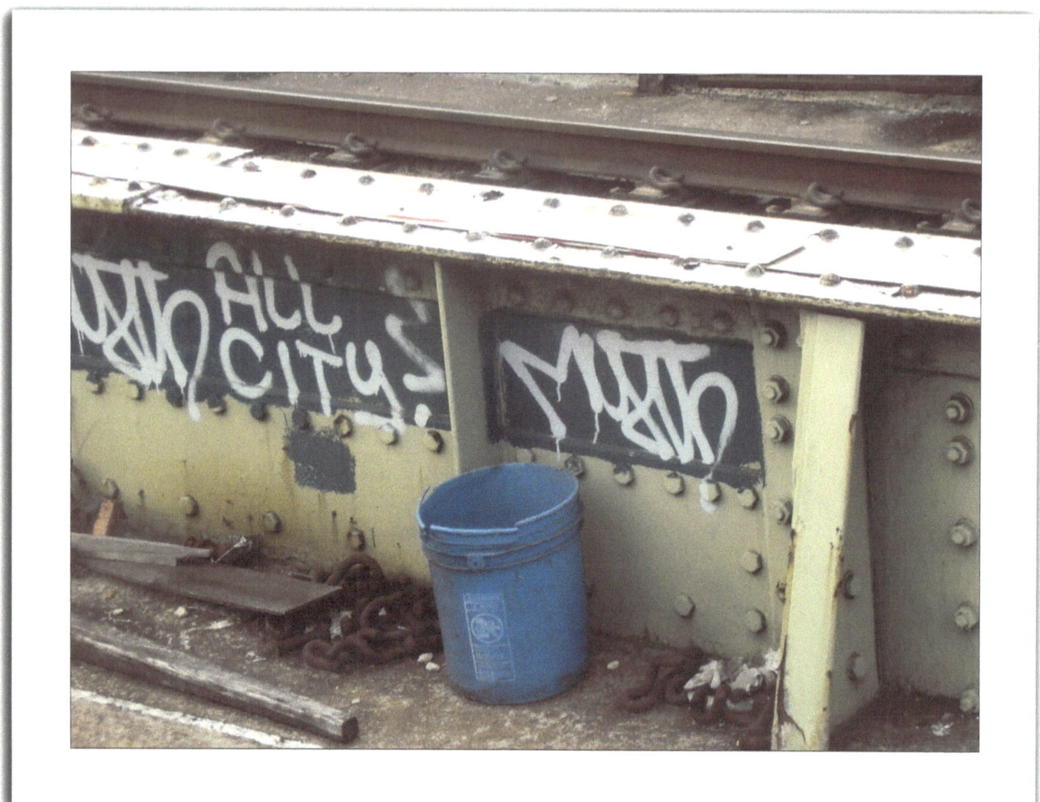

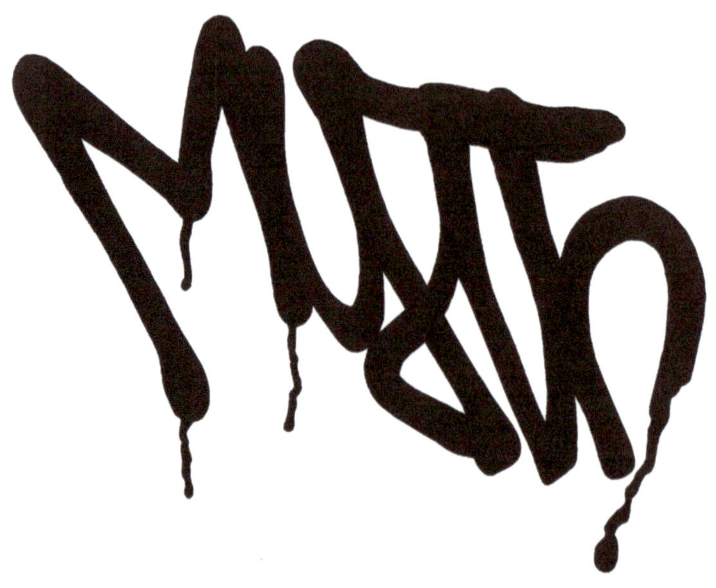

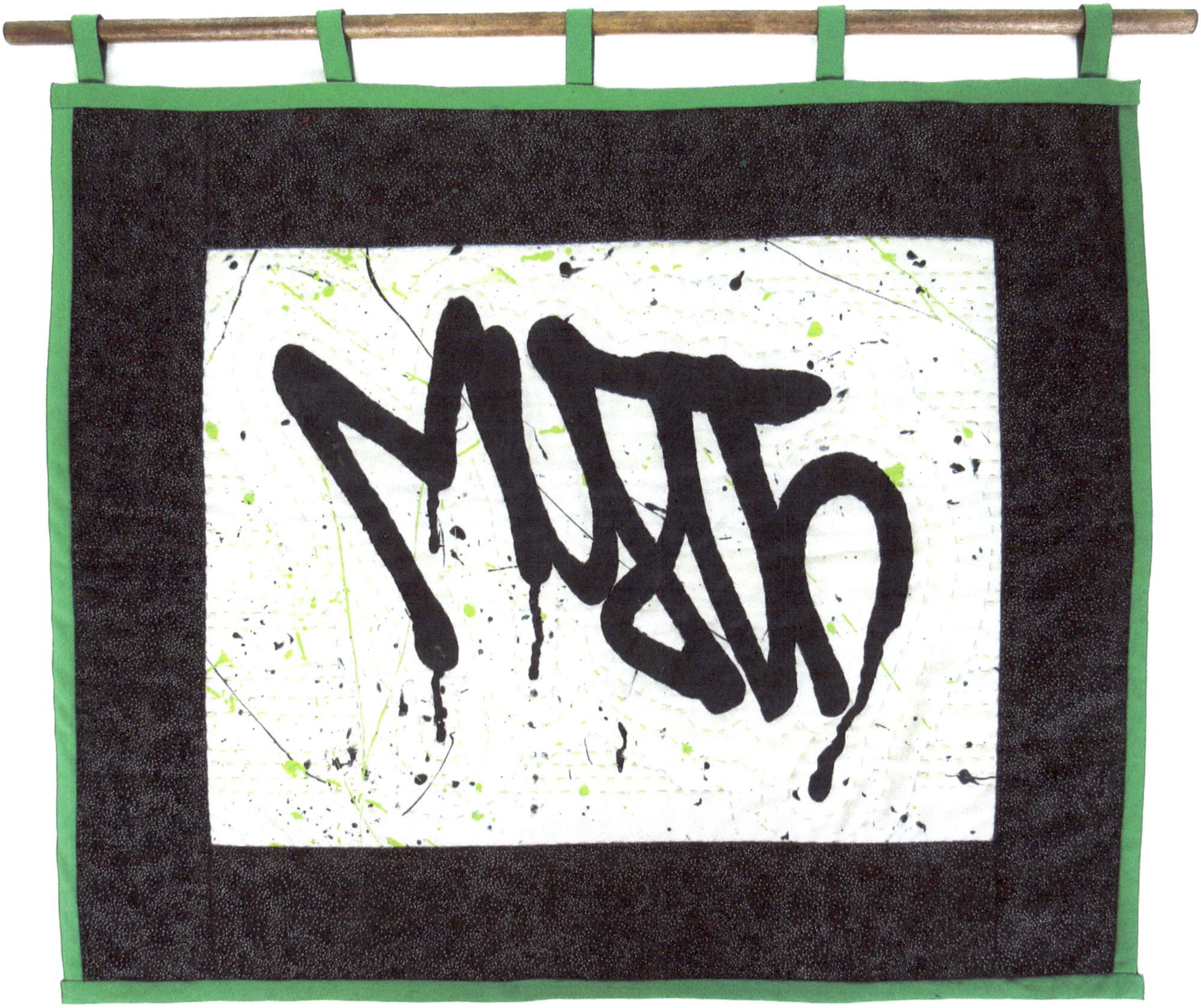

NOTE: Striped green fabric underneath the grey gives this quilt added color.

Finished Quilt Size: 18” x 21 1/2”
Border: 3”
Binding: Double-Fold, Extra-Wide Bias Tape
Back: 18” x 21 1/2” Scrap Fabric

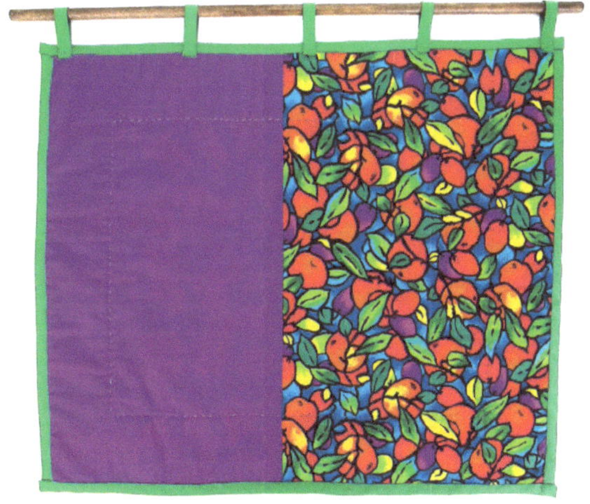

NOW WHAT

Abandoned Winery - Fountaingrove, California

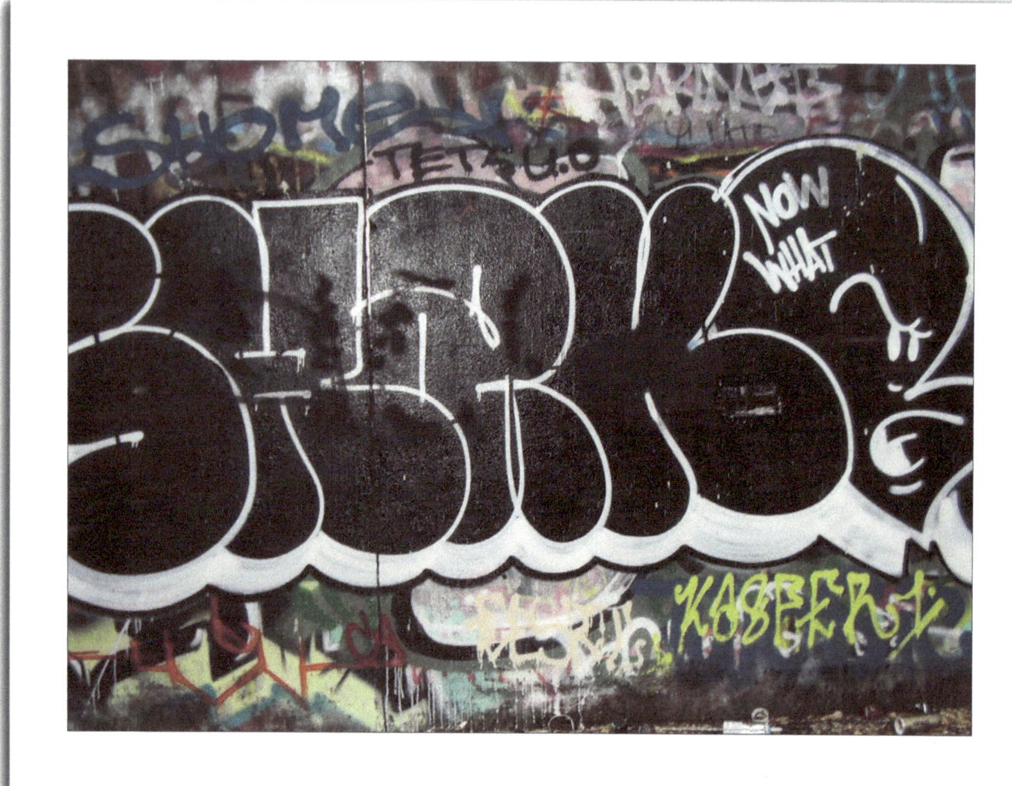

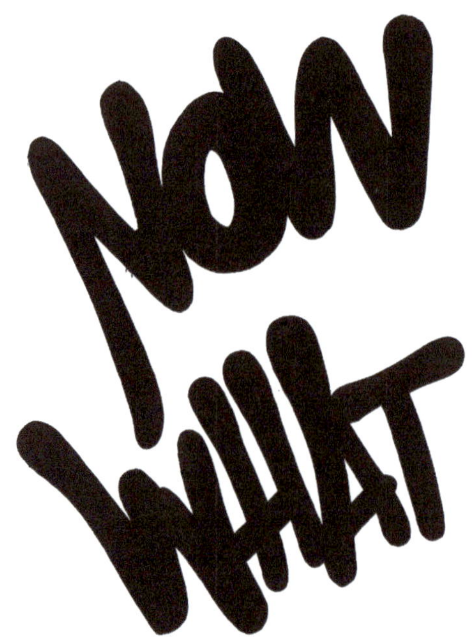

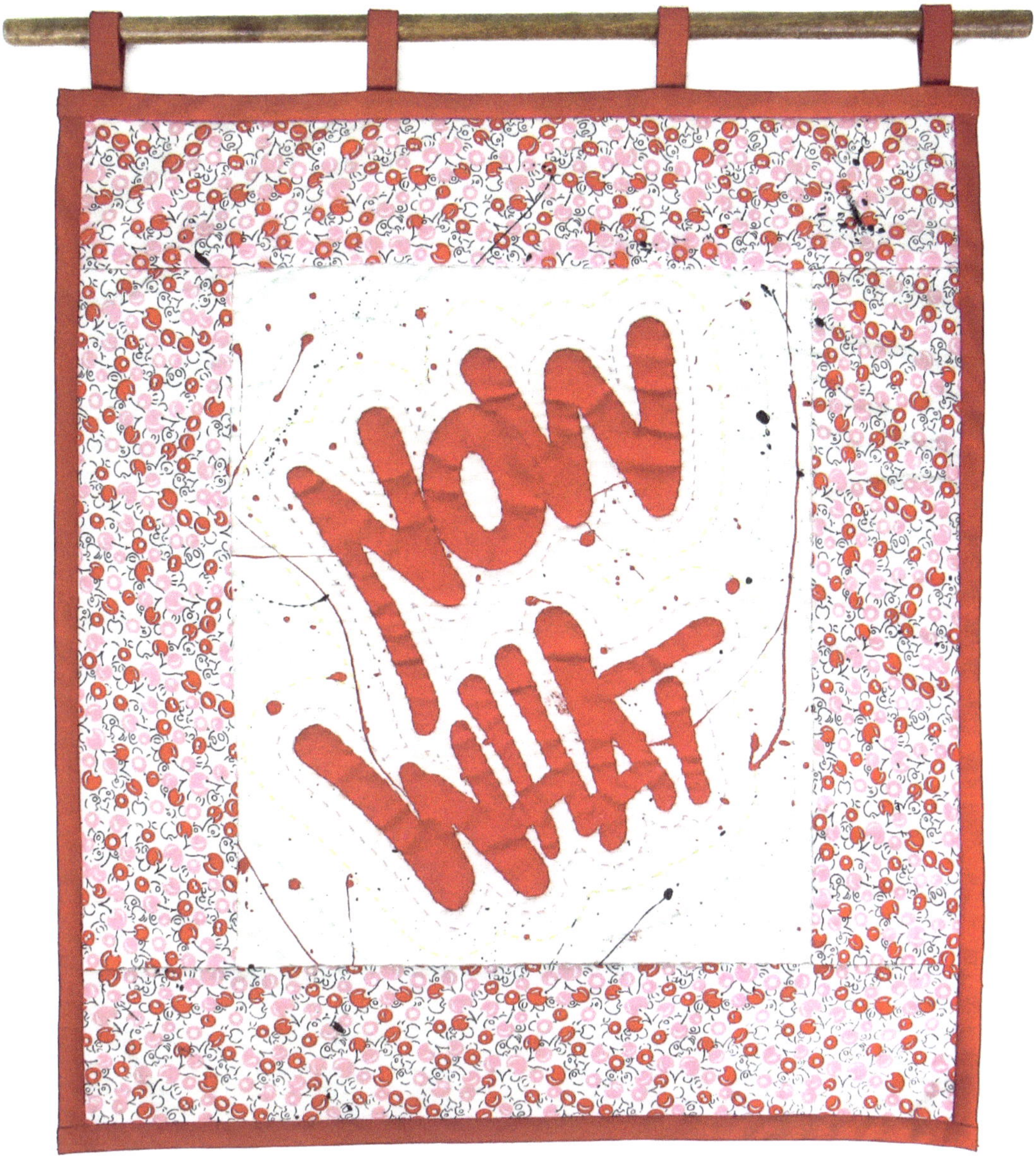

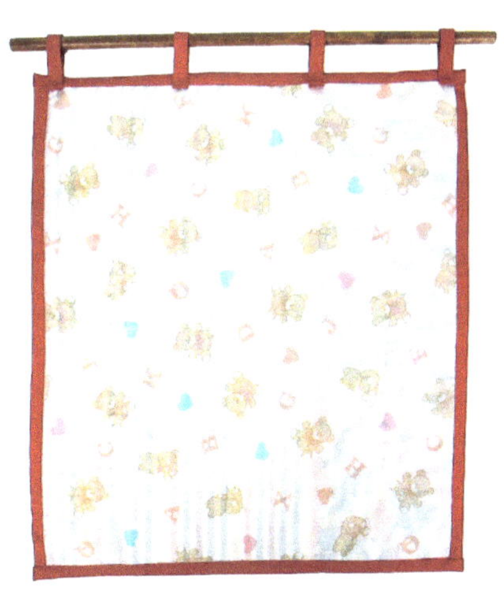

NOTE: You never know where you will find inspiration. Rule - photograph everything!

Finished Quilt Size: 17 3/4" x 16"
Border: 3"
Binding: Double-Fold, Extra-Wide Bias Tape
Back: 17 3/4" x 16" Scrap Fabric

LOGIC

Store Wall - Brooklyn, New York City

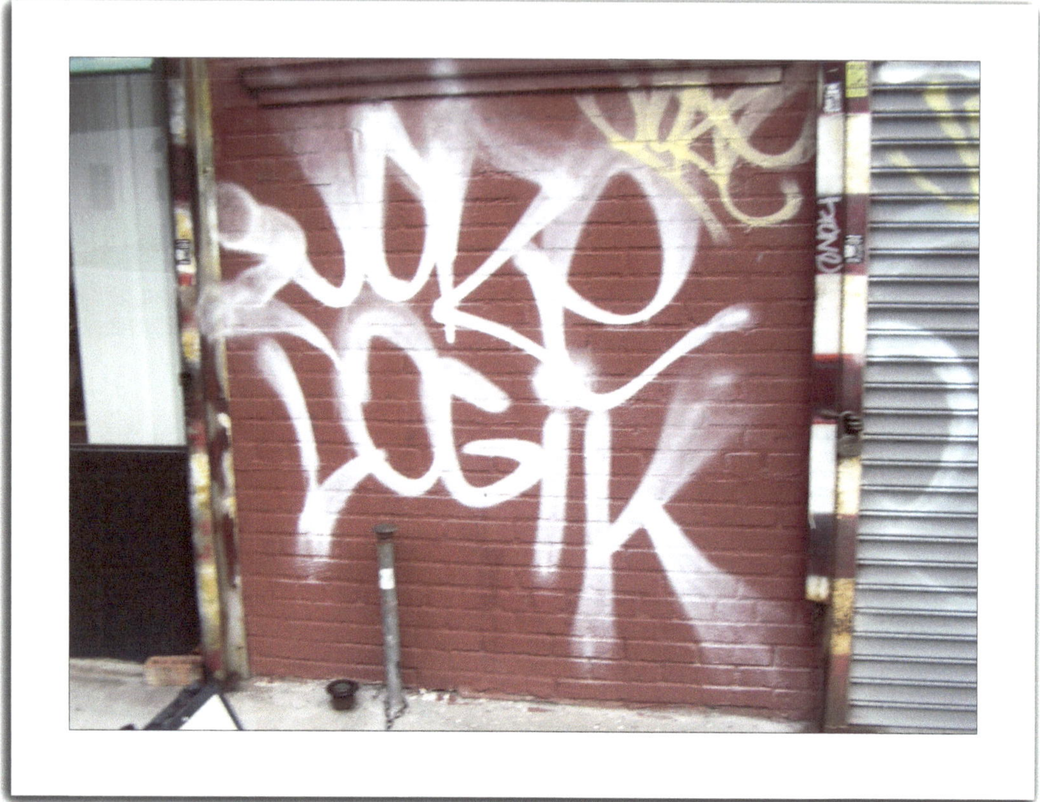

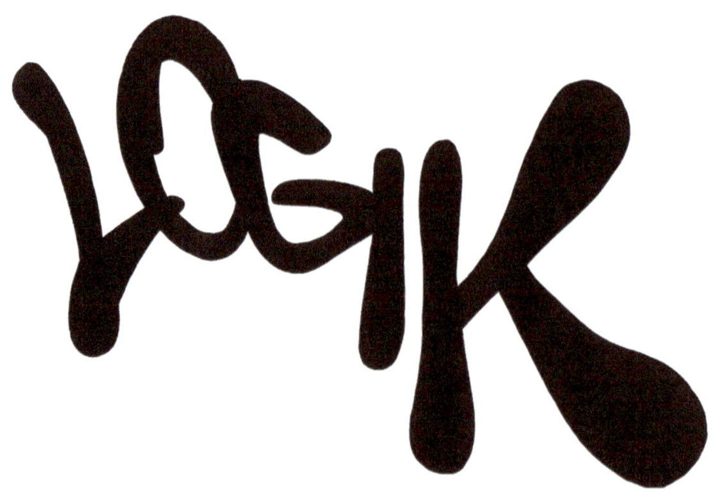

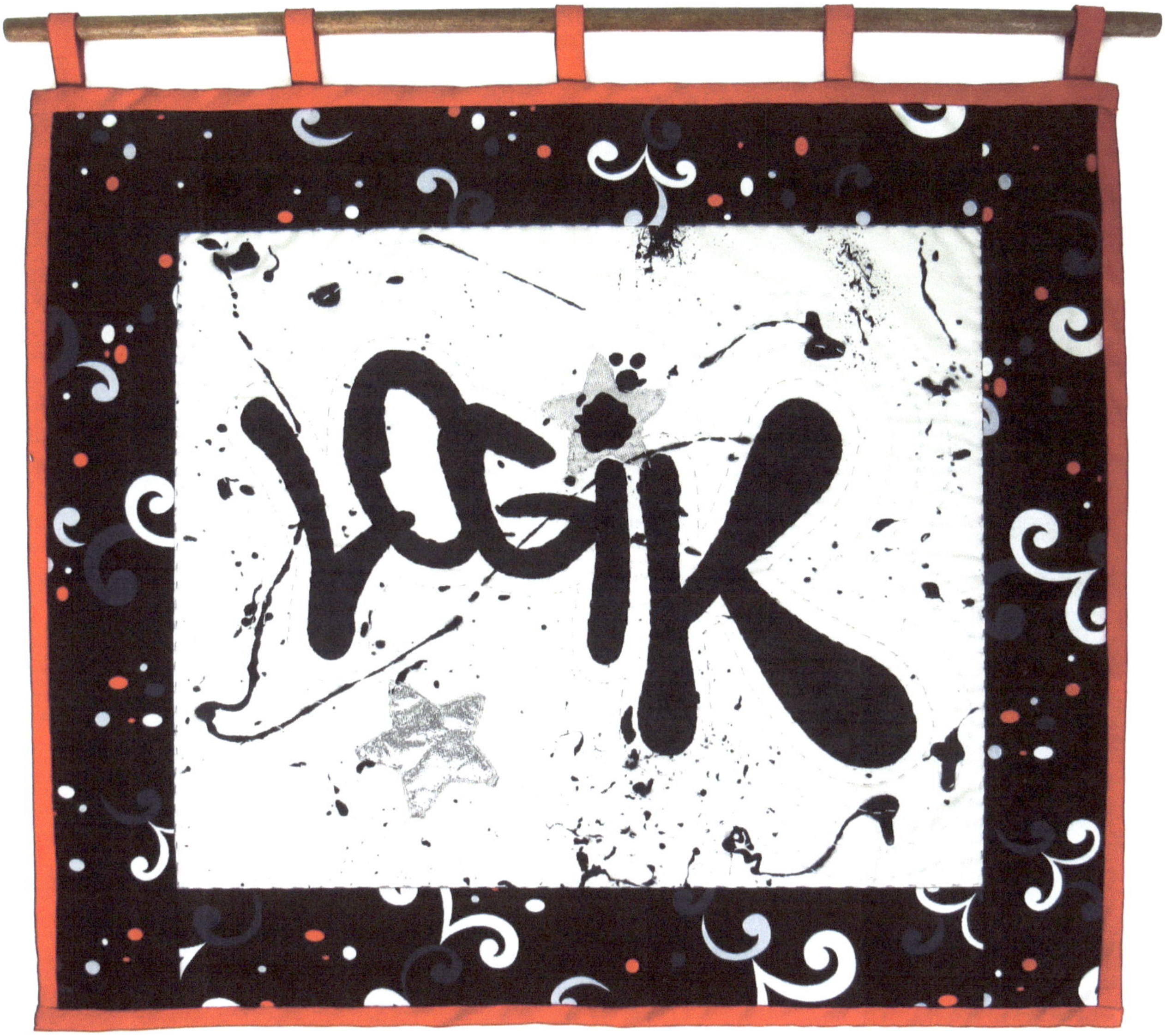

NOTE: This quilt has silver and black tulle star appliqués. It was the first one I made so it's a bit messy.

Finished Quilt Size: 18" x 22 1/2"
Border: 2 1/2"
Binding: Double-Fold, Extra-Wide Bias Tape
Back: 18" x 22 1/2" Scrap Fabric

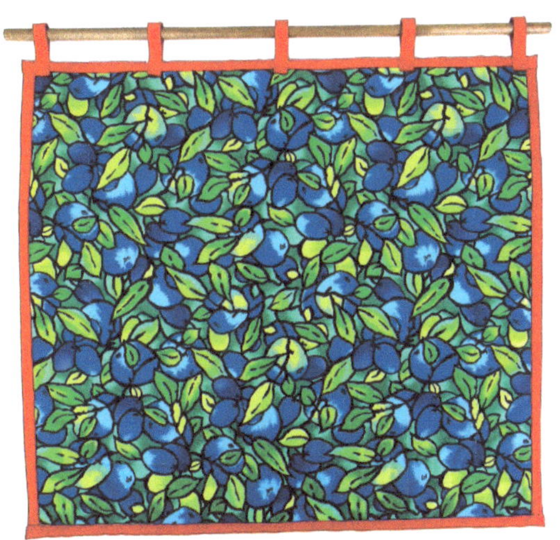

'K' WITH ARROW

Construction Site Fence - Brighton Beach, New York City

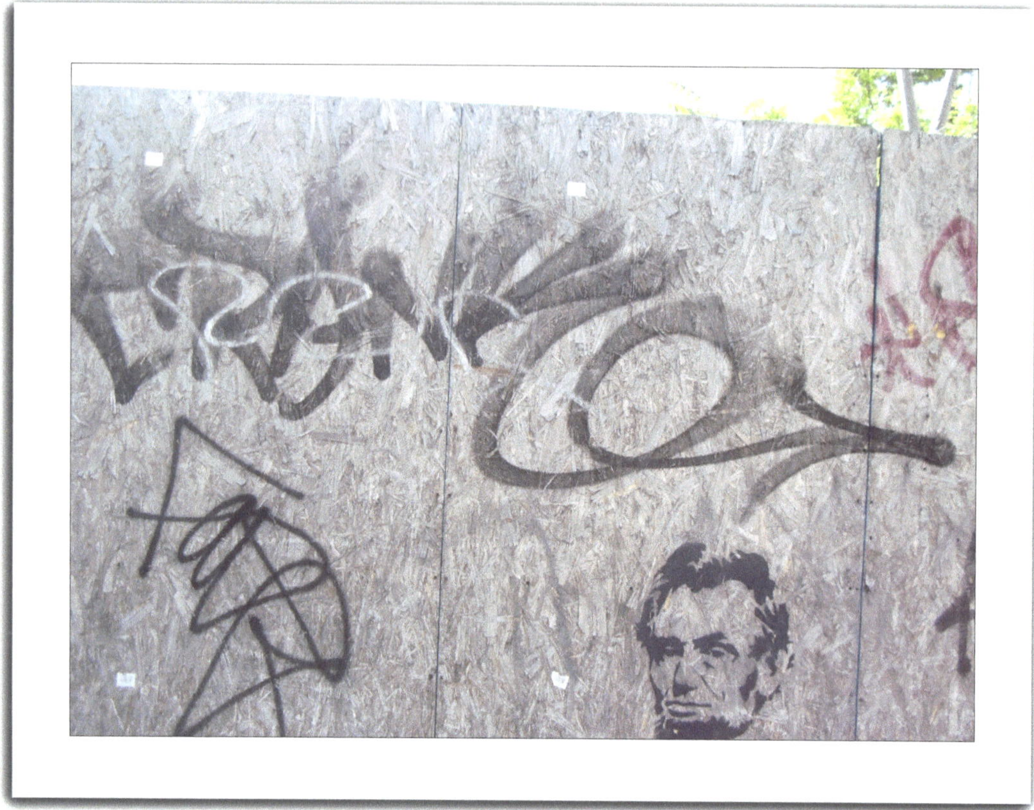

This tag says CRANK. I thought it would be fun to experiment with just the letter 'K' which has a great arrow on the end.

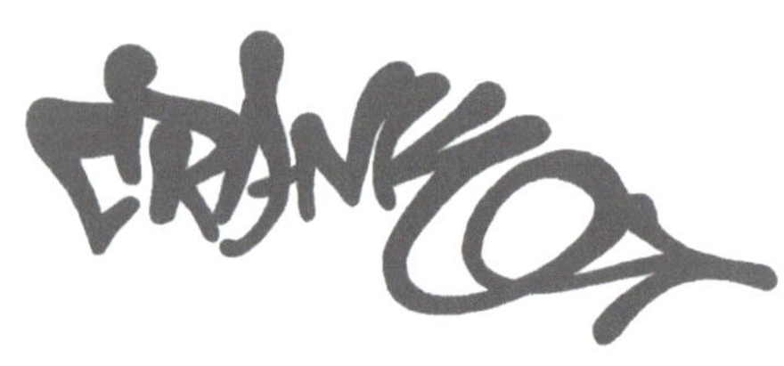

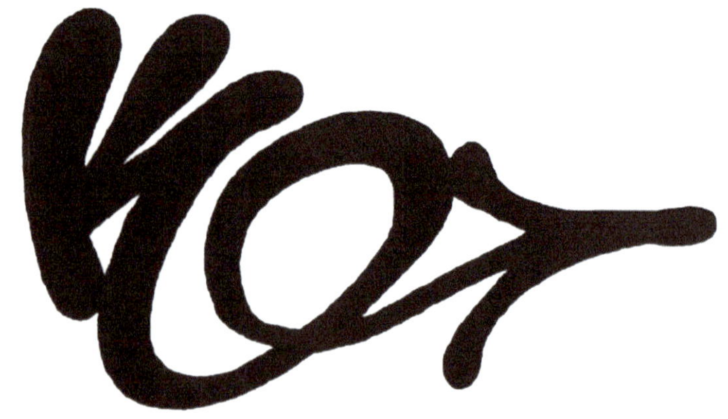

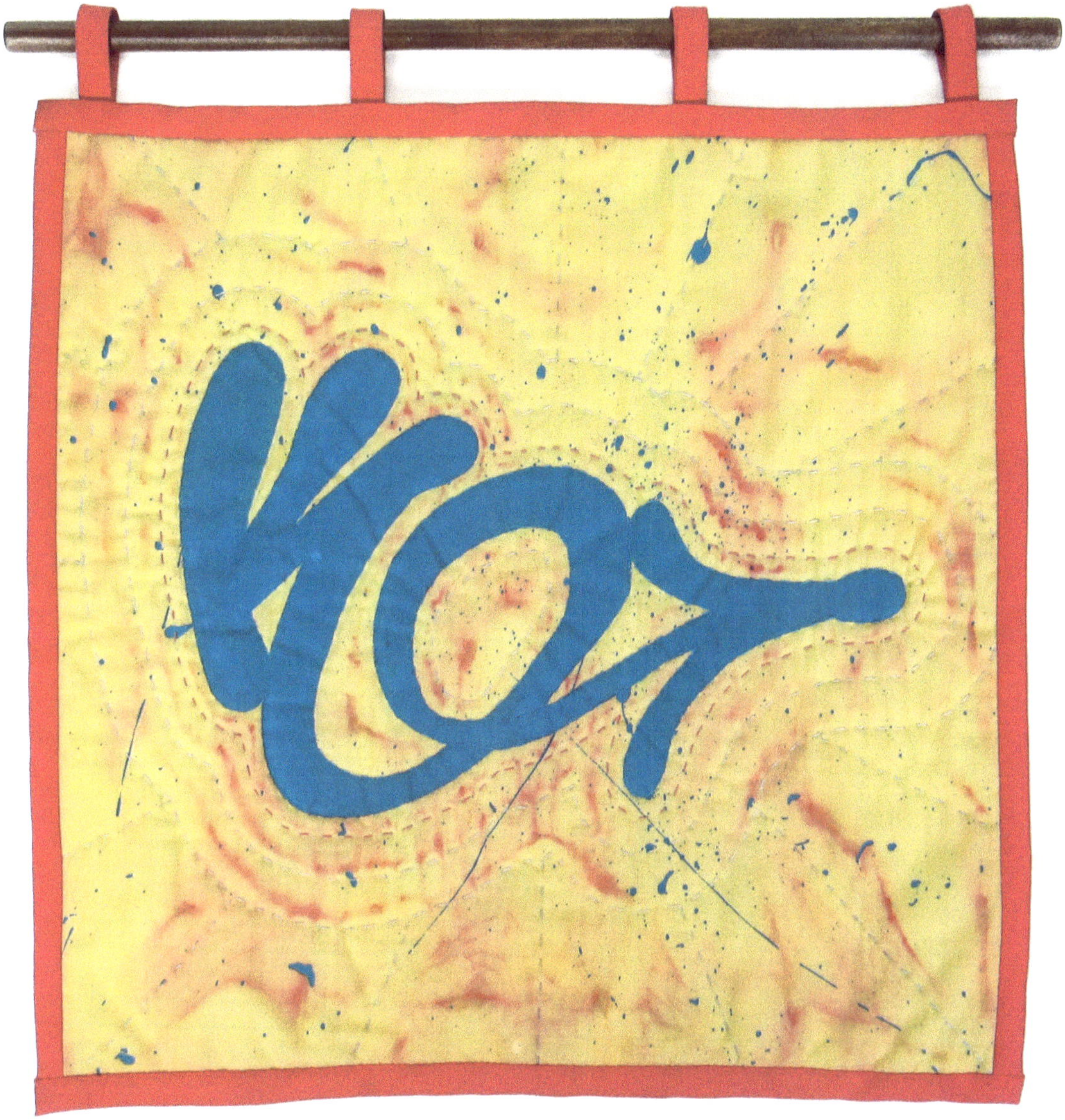

NOTE: A great alphabet quilt for a kids room. The red back fabric bled when I tried to wash this quilt and created a tie-dye effect! No border necessary.

Finished Quilt Size: 14" x 14"
Border: none
Binding: Double-Fold, Extra-Wide Bias Tape
Back: 14" x 14" Scrap Fabric

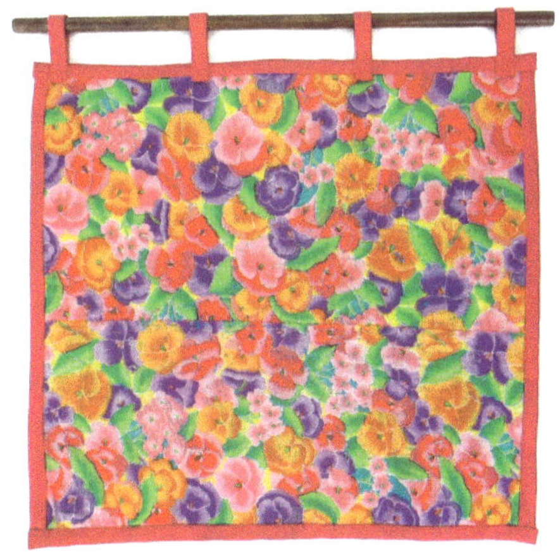

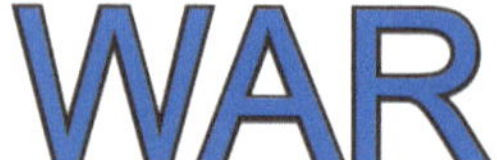

What's it good for?

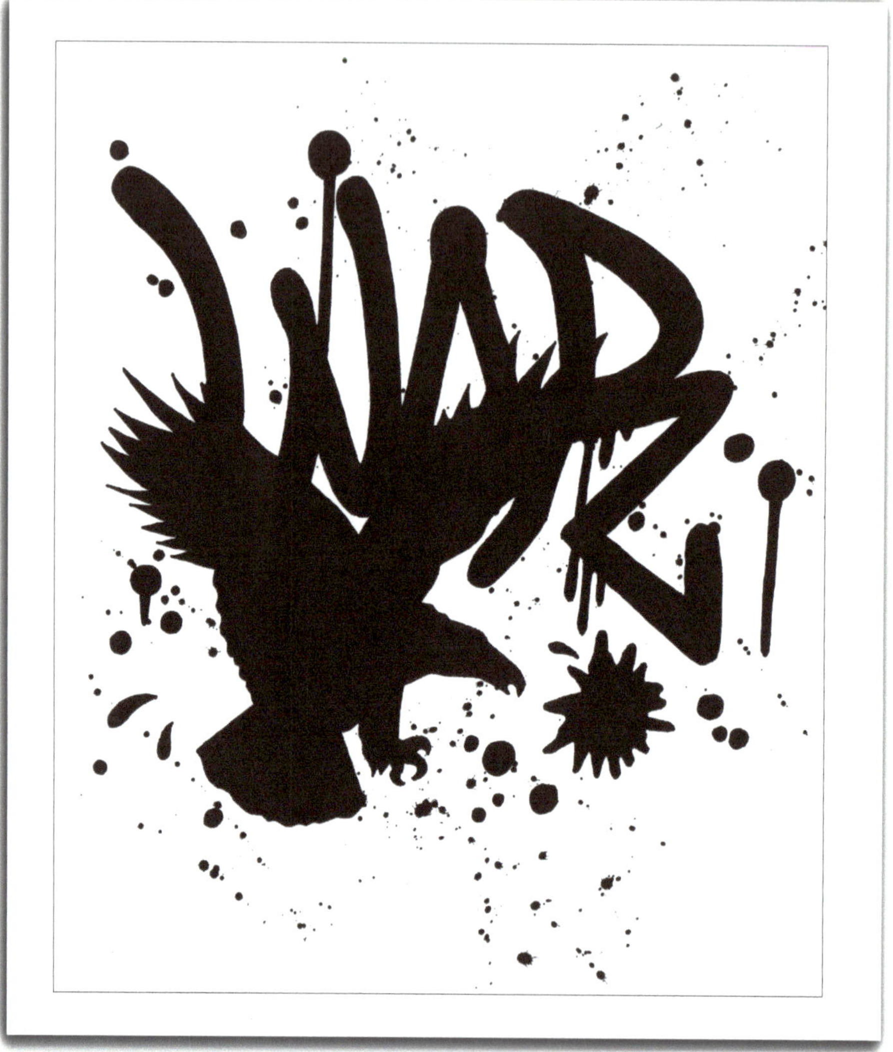

Embroider words and other details with metallic thread over a paint pen.

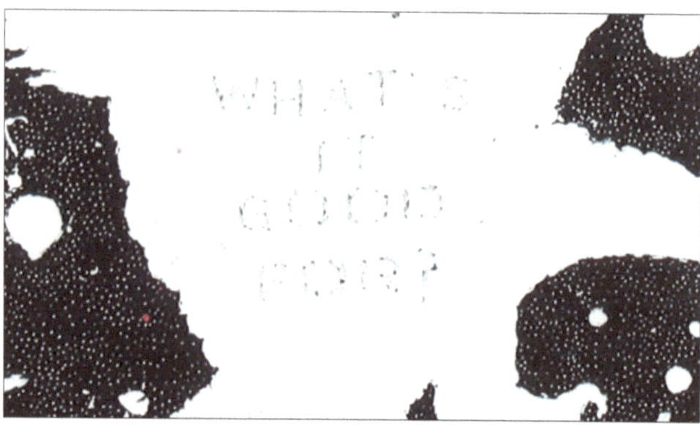

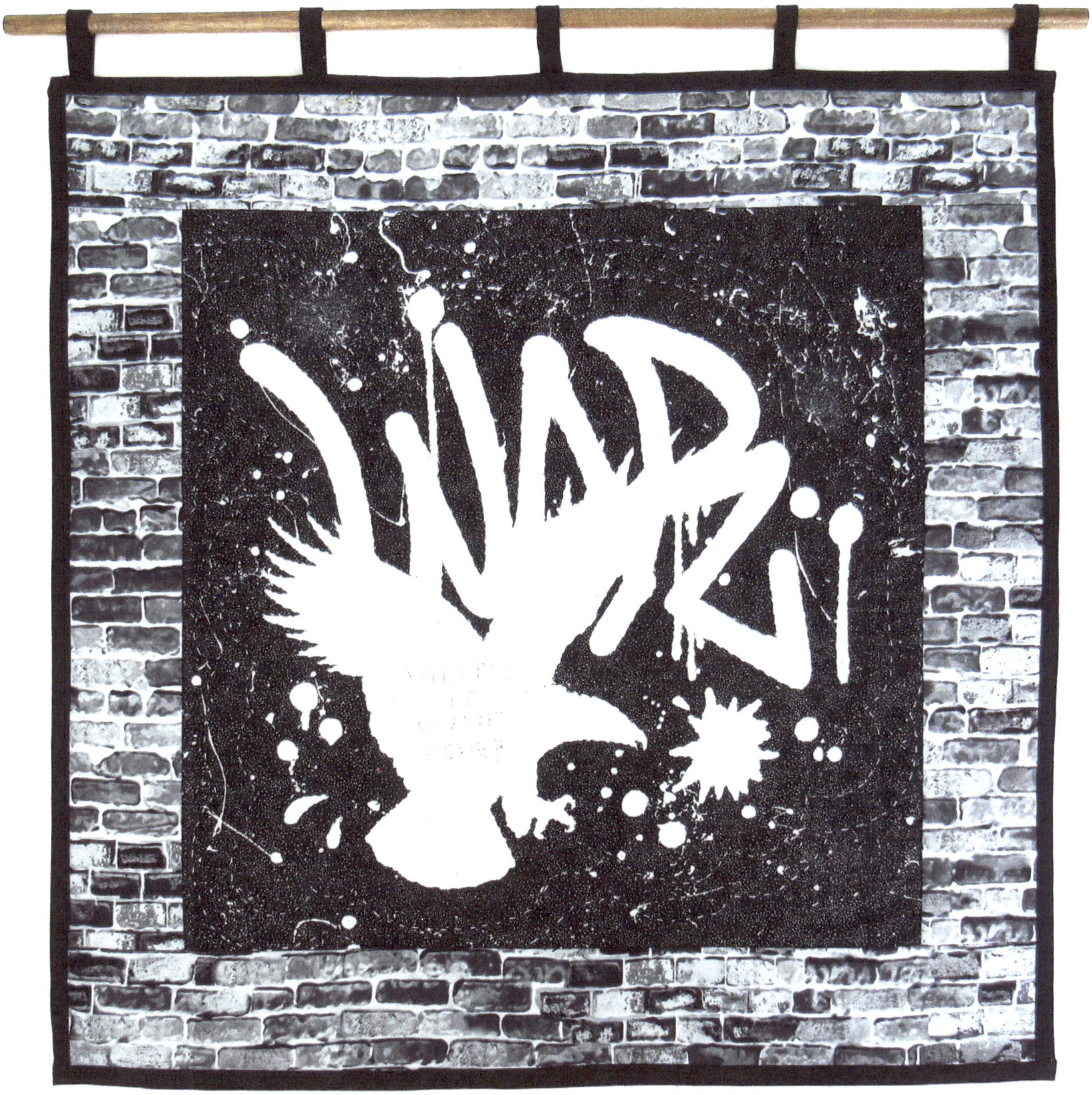

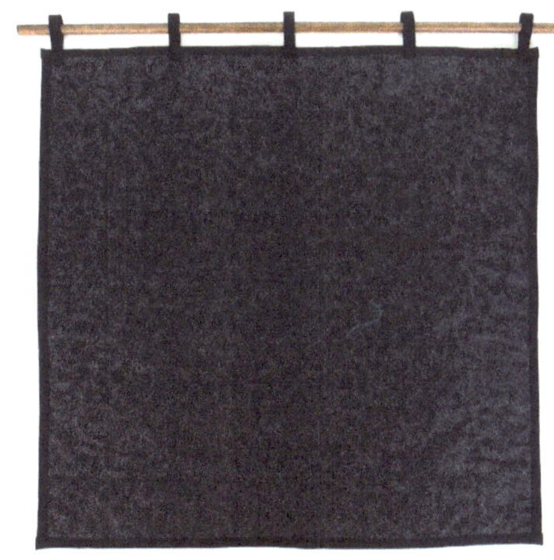

Finished Quilt Size: 21 1/2" x 22 1/2"
Border: 3"
Binding: Double-Fold, Extra-Wide Bias Tape
Back: 21 1/2" x 22 1/2" Scrap Fabric

PEACE

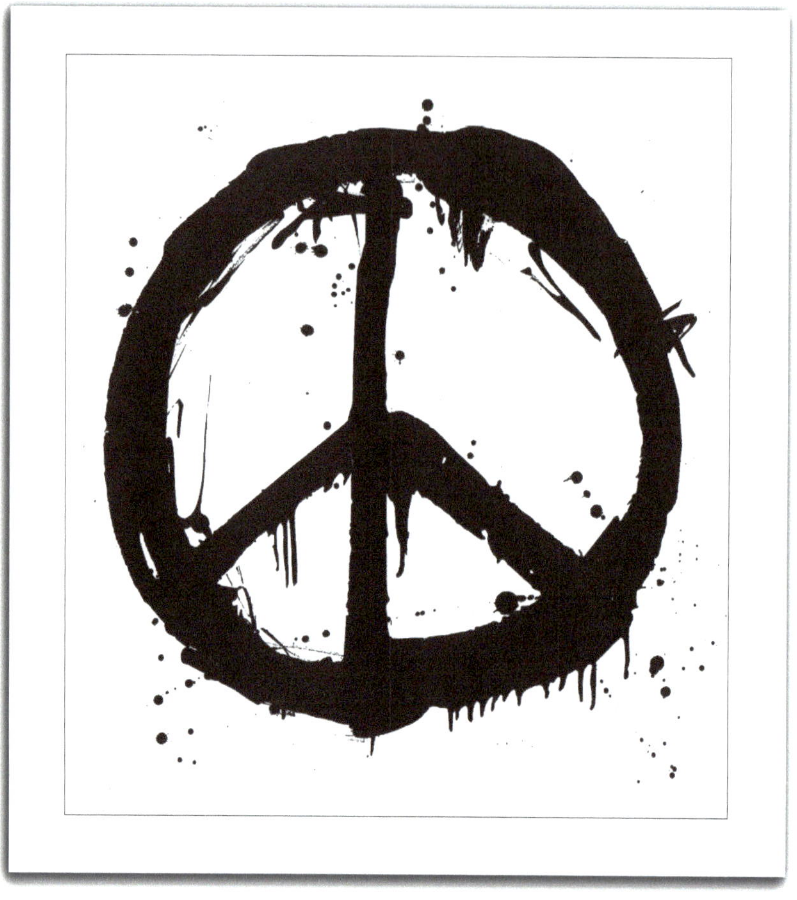

Quilt around and around your painted symbol as many times as you like. Use matching threads, contrasting bright colors, or metallic threads.

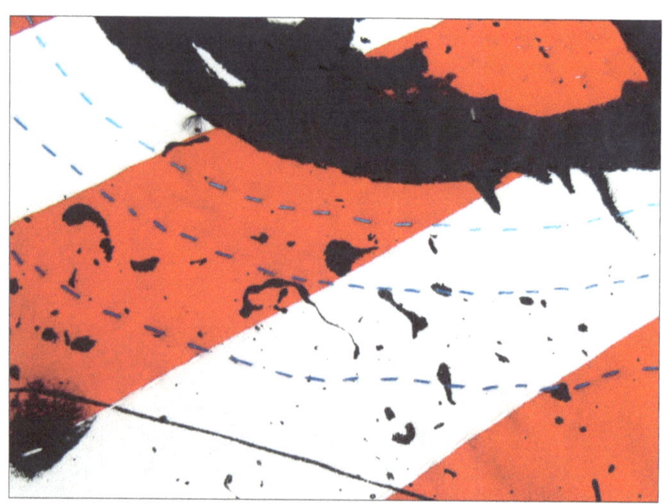

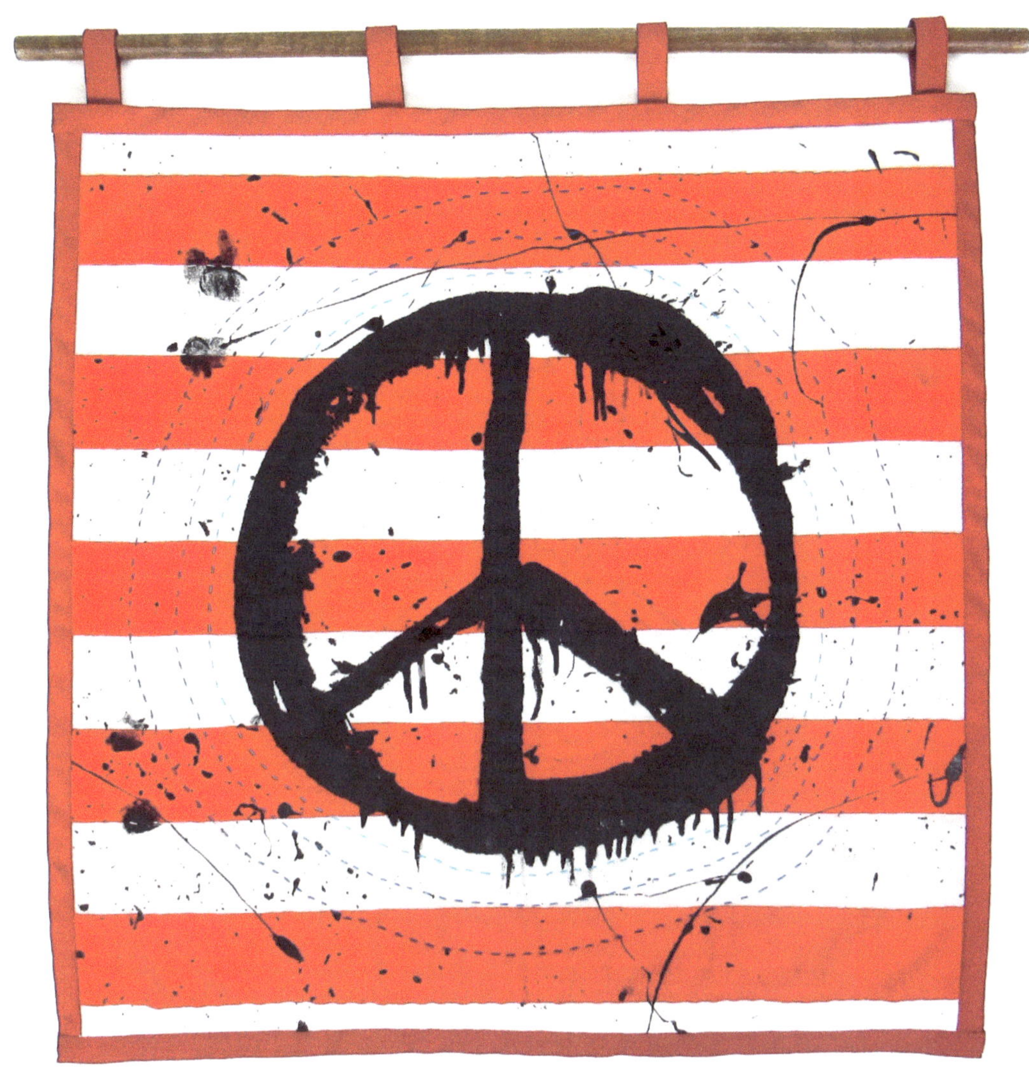

NOTES: Paint any symbol on printed fabric and quilt the drips and splashes. No border necessary.

Finished Quilt Size: 16 1/2" x 16 1/2"
Border: none
Binding: Double-Fold, Extra-Wide Bias Tape
Back: 16 1/2" x 16 1/2" Scrap Fabric

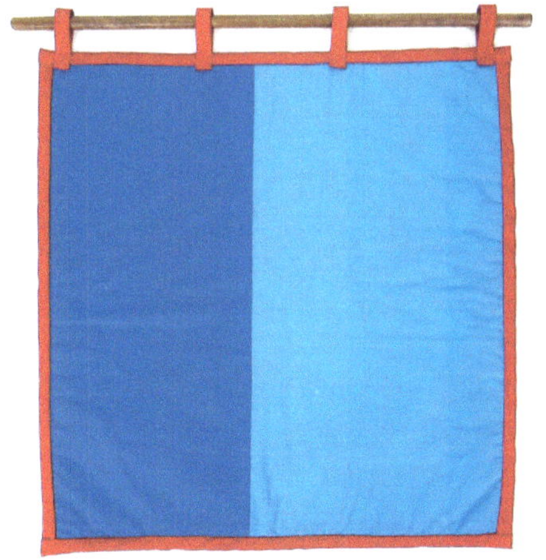

INSTRUCTIONS TO MAKE A MINI QUILT

1. All fabrics should be 100% cotton or a poly-cotton blend.
2. Wash and dry all fabrics to pre-shrink and remove fabric stiffener (called *sizing*) before use.
3. You can buy fabric paint in art or craft stores, or substitute with liquid acrylic paint.
4. Adult supervision is needed if using an iron to heatset fabric paint.
5. Cover painted areas with a cloth when pressing to prevent paint from sticking to your iron.
6. Double-Fold, Extra-Wide Bias Tape works best for binding, but use whatever size you like.
7. Mini quilts can be made completely by hand, with a sewing machine, or a combination of both.
8. A thimble is your friend. Learn to use one. Or three.

STEP 1: DRAWING A TAG

OPTION A

This is the simplest option.

Create or find a tag you like. Draw it with a black magic marker on a white piece of paper that is approximately 14" x 17". You are ready to paint on fabric. Go to Page 42.

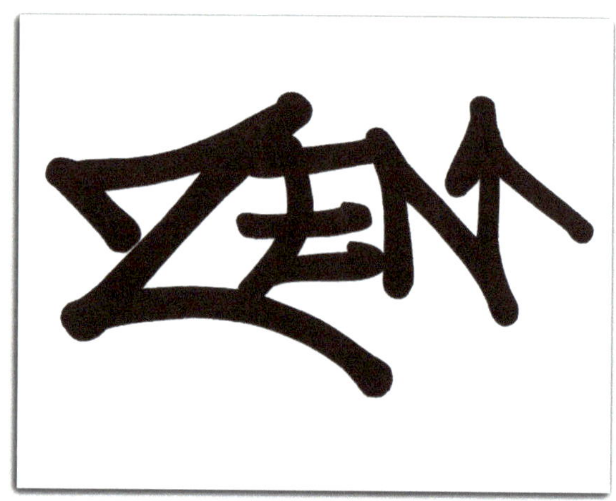

Approximately 14" x 17"

OPTION B

Draw your tag on a giant piece of paper as large as you can get. A roll of white paper works great. Or a large pad of drawing paper 19" x 24". Or newsprint paper.

When your tag is done take a photograph. Download the photograph to your computer.

Print the tag out on an 8 1/2" x 11" piece of white copy paper. Go to STEP 2: ENLARGING A TAG.

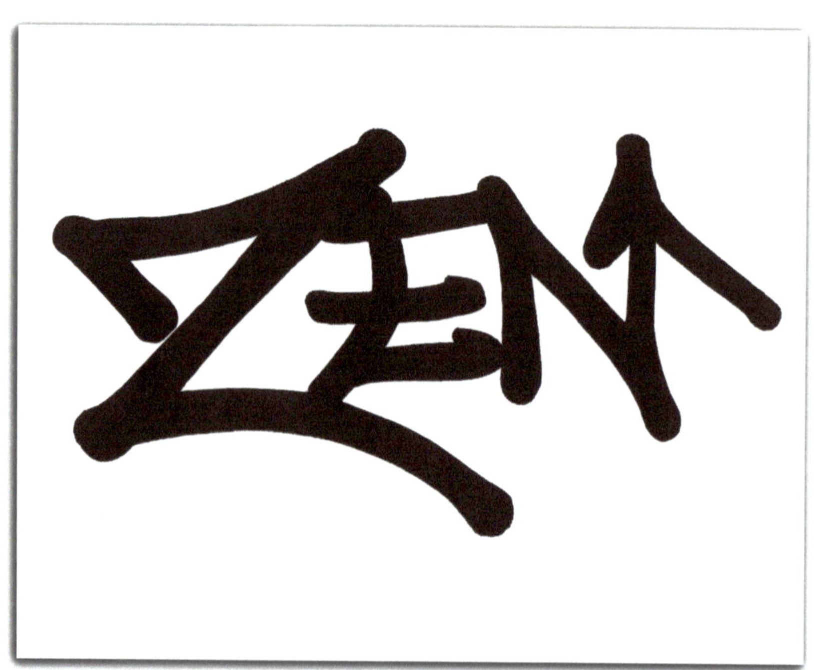

19" x 24" or Larger

OPTION C

Draw your tag directly on an 8 1/2" x 11" piece of copy paper. Go to STEP 2: ENLARGING A TAG.

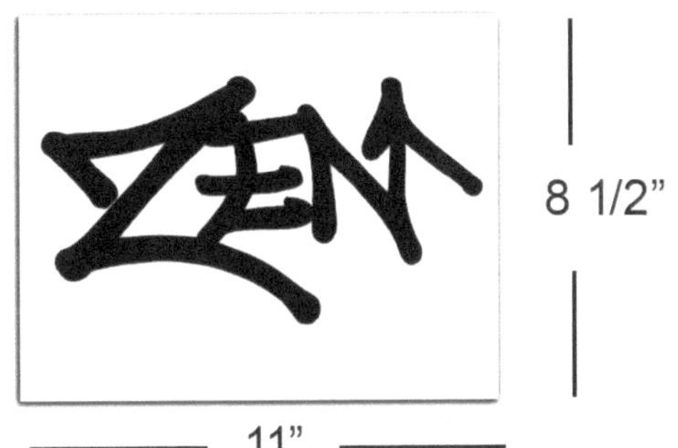

STEP 2: ENLARGING A TAG

1. Starting with your tag on an 8 1/2" x 11" piece of paper, draw a line down the middle of the tag.

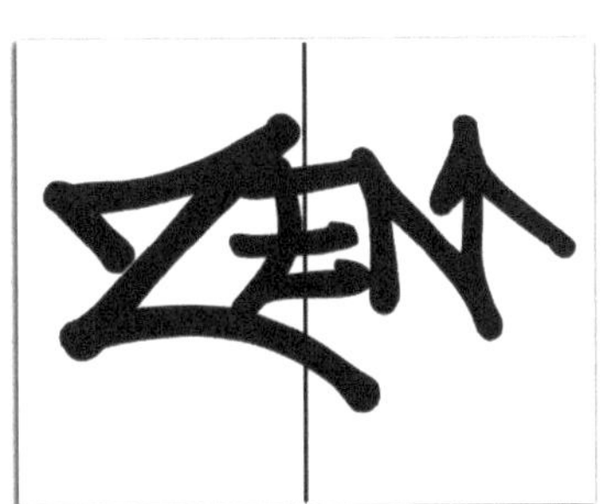

2. Cut the page in half along the middle line.

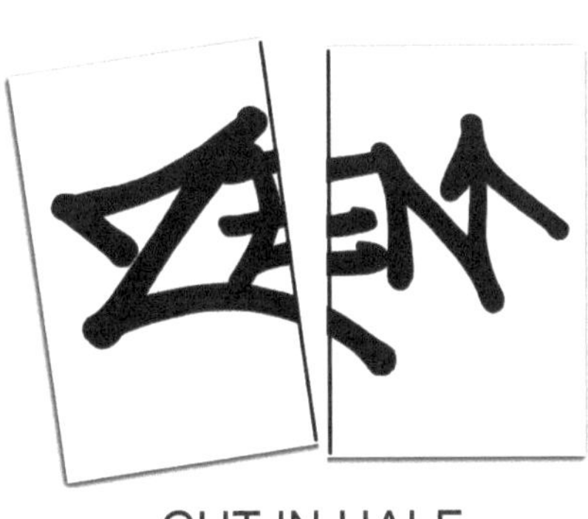

CUT IN HALF

3. Scan each half separately into your computer. Enlarge each half of the tag so that it fills up an 8 1/2" x 11" piece of paper. Print both halves.

4. Join the two halves together at the middle line. Tape and/or glue in place. Your tag will now be twice as big, on a piece of paper that is approximately 11" x 17".

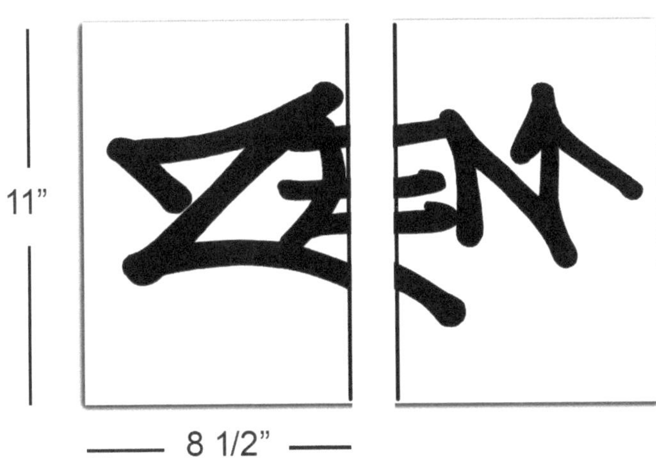

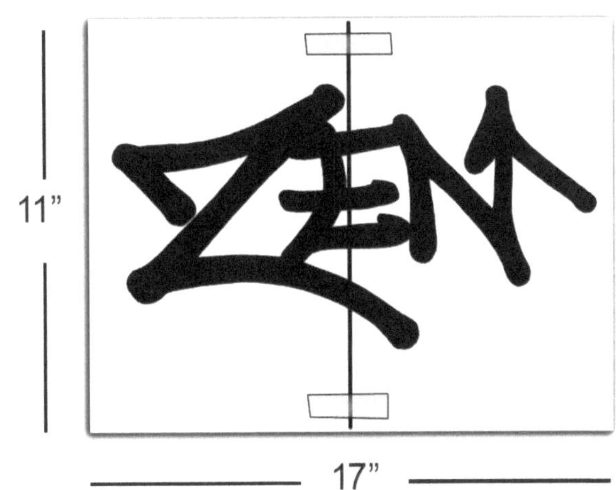

PAINTING THE TAG ON FABRIC FOR THE QUILT TOP

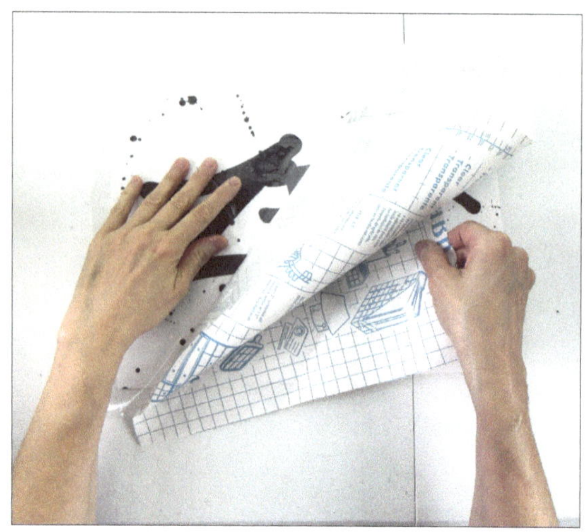

1. Cut a piece of clear contact paper that measures 1/2" larger all around than your paper. Peel off a corner of the backing paper. Starting at one corner, carefully cover the tag with the contact paper. Remove the backing paper completely. Press out any air bubbles. Fold the extra edges of contact paper over to the backside. The contact paper will prevent the fabric from sticking to the paper when it is wet with paint.

2. Tape the tag design down firmly to a piece of cardboard or canvas board. The board should be about 3" wider than the paper all the way around.

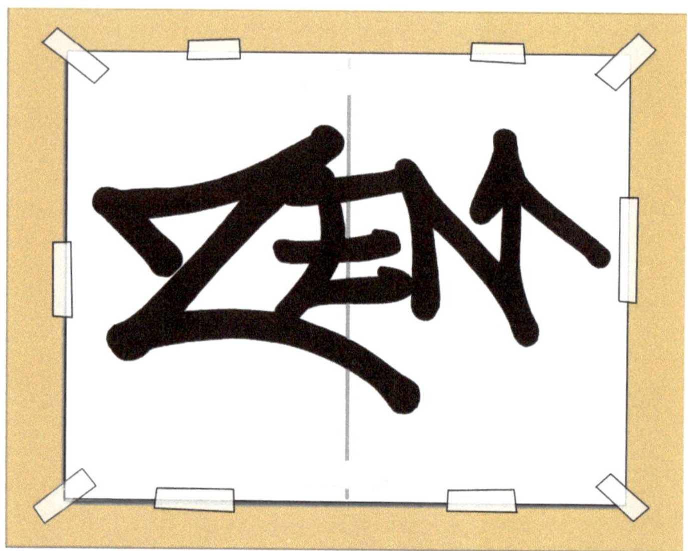

3. Lay a piece of light colored fabric over the tag design. A 100% cotton fabric or a poly-cotton blend works best. The fabric needs to be just thin enough so you can see the tag through the fabric. Tape the edges of the fabric down all the way around. You can use Blue Carpenter's Tape or Masking Tape.

TAG SHOWS THROUGH FABRIC

4. Trace the tag outline lightly with a pencil. This outline will make it easier to paint the tag if your fabric shifts slightly later on.

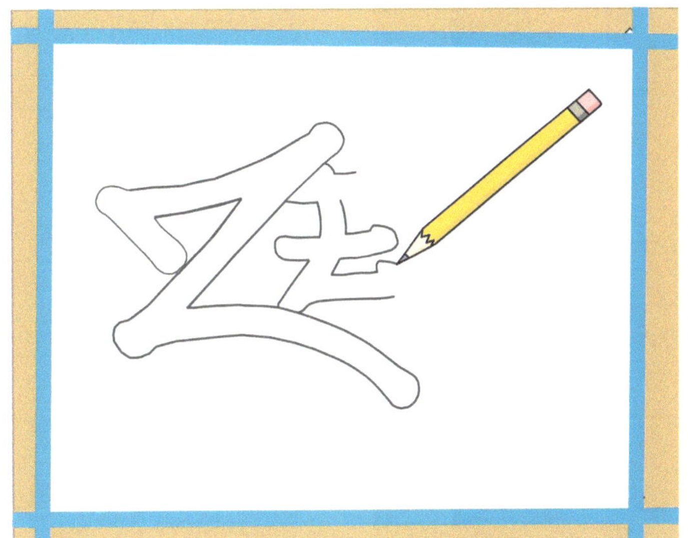

5. Paint in the tag with fabric paint.

NOTE: If you decide to use a light colored paint on a dark colored fabric, you will need to use a lightbox to see the tag through the fabric. Or just paint the tag freehand, whichever works best for you. I prefer to use a lightbox.

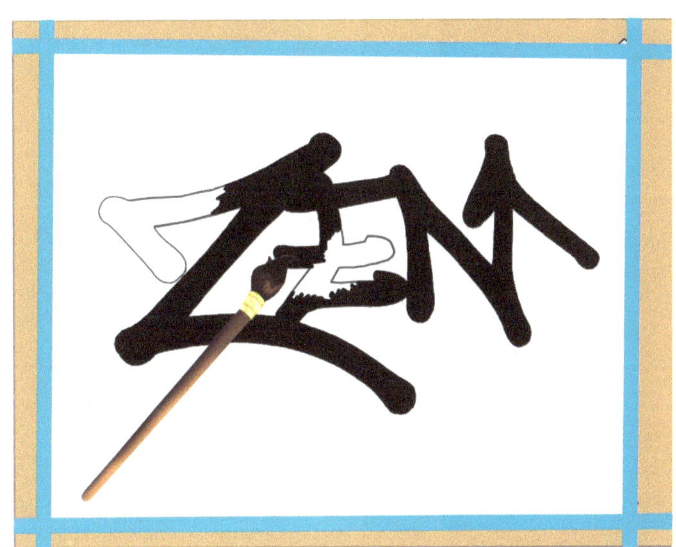

6. Make a splash and splatter design over the tag with a paint brush and the fabric paint. You can also use an eyedropper to make big drops and a toothbrush to make tiny drops. Practice your technique on a piece of scrap paper first until you feel confident.

7. Let the paint dry for an hour and then carefully remove the fabric from the board. It will stick a little bit. Remove the paper drawing from the board and lay the painted fabric out on the board. Put it aside to dry. When dry, **HEATSET** following the manufacturer's directions on the jar of paint you are using. This is your quilt top.

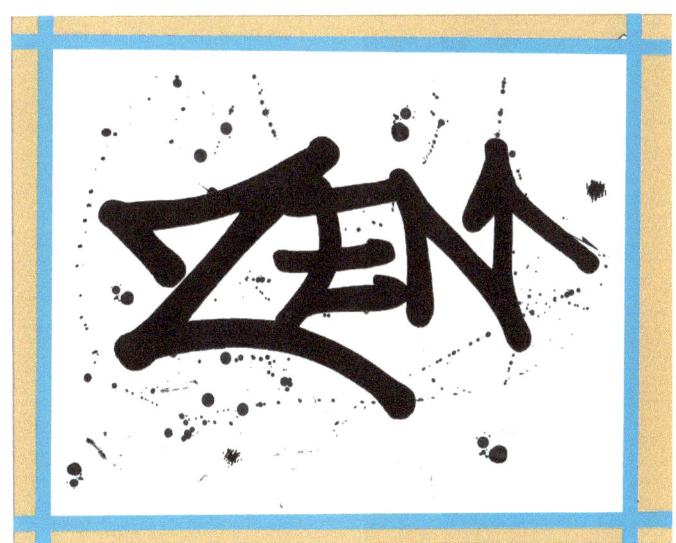

ADDING BORDERS AND QUILTING THE QUILT TOP

The border fabric is important because it will be used to frame your tag. A brightly colored print or dark color will make your quilt look more dramatic. Don't use a print that is too busy or it will compete for attention with the tag design.

1. Trim the quilt top (painted panel) down to the size you want. Make sure the corners are as squared as possible.

Measure the width of the quilt top from side to side. Cut two strips of border fabric that are the width of the quilt top x 3 1/2" wide.

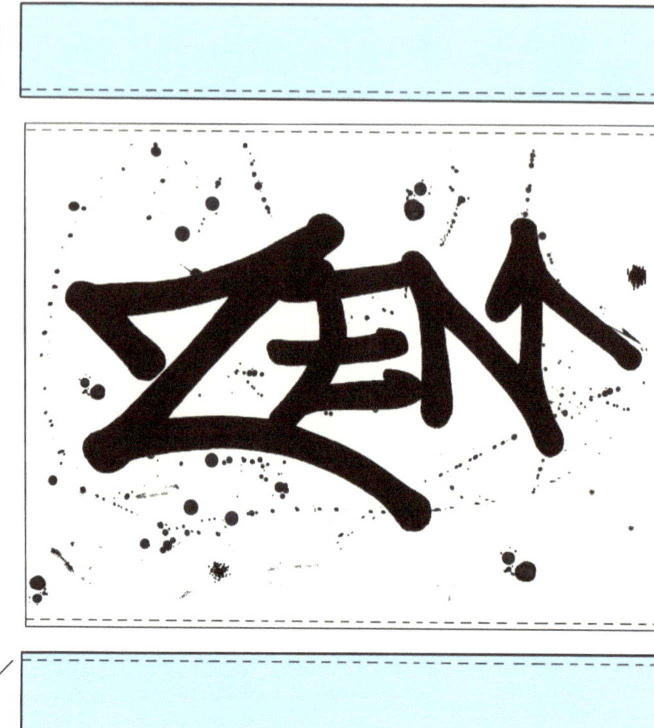

3 1/2" x width of quilt top

1/4" SEAM ALLOWANCE

2. Sew the border strips to the top and bottom of the quilt top with 1/4" seam allowance. Turn over to the back and press seams behind the border fabric.

NOTE: Seam allowance is the area between the raw edge of the fabric and the stitching line.

OPTION: If you want to make the border strips wider or thinner that is totally up to you. This is just a general size that I use.

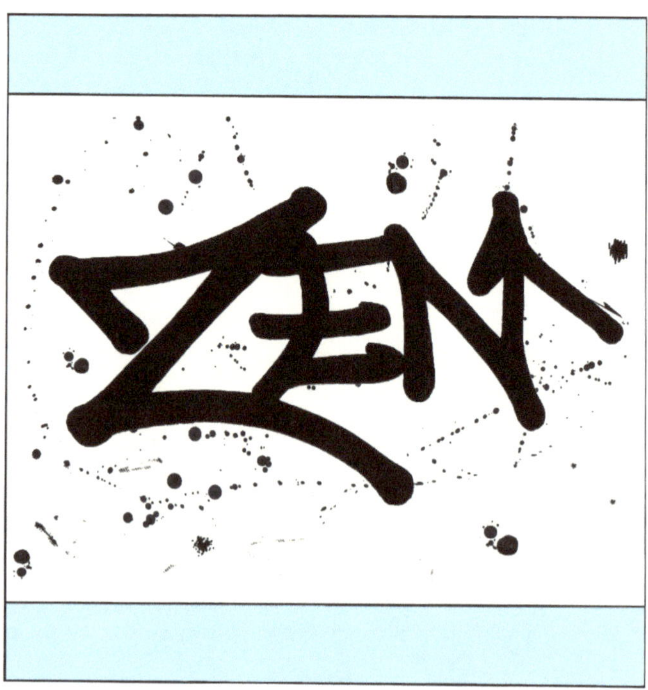

3. Measure the height of the quilt top from top to bottom including the attached border strips. Cut two strips of border fabric measuring the height of the quilt top x 3 1/2" wide.

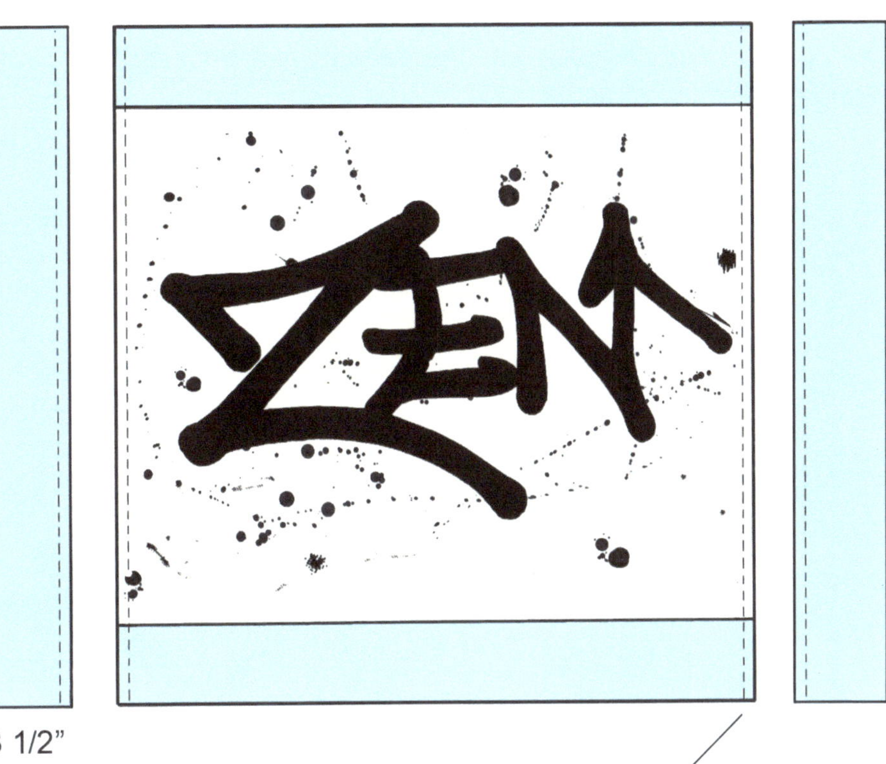

1/4" SEAM ALLOWANCE

3 1/2" x height of quilt top

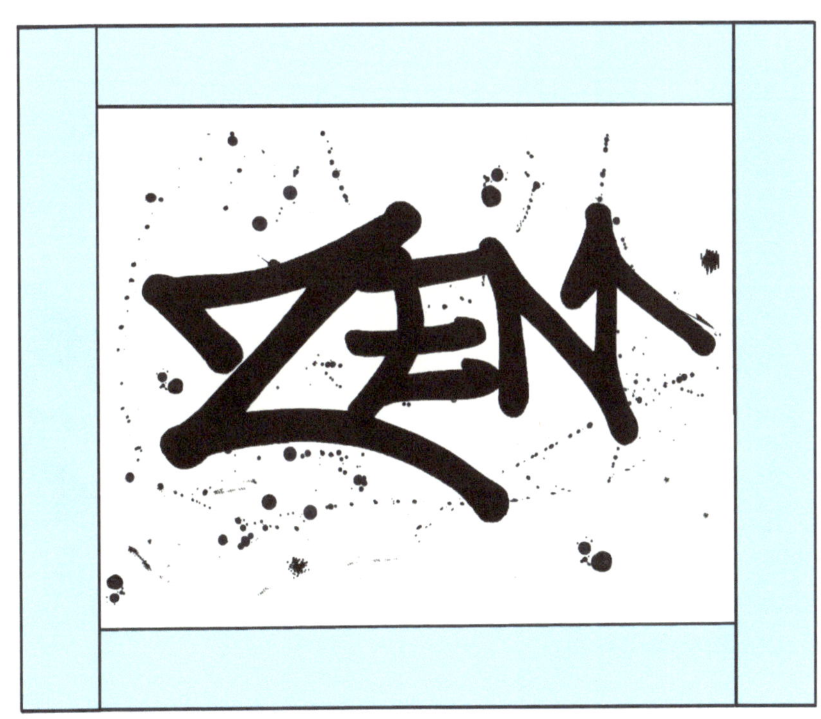

4. Sew the strips of border fabric to both sides of the quilt top with 1/4" seam allowance. Turn over to the back and press seams behind the border fabric.

NOTE: Pressing the seams behind the darker colored border fabric will prevent these seams from showing through the front of the quilt.

5. Cut a piece of quilt batting the same size as the quilt top plus 1" all around. Cut a piece of backing fabric the same size as the batting. This backing fabric will be hidden inside the quilt when finished so it doesn't need to be anything special.

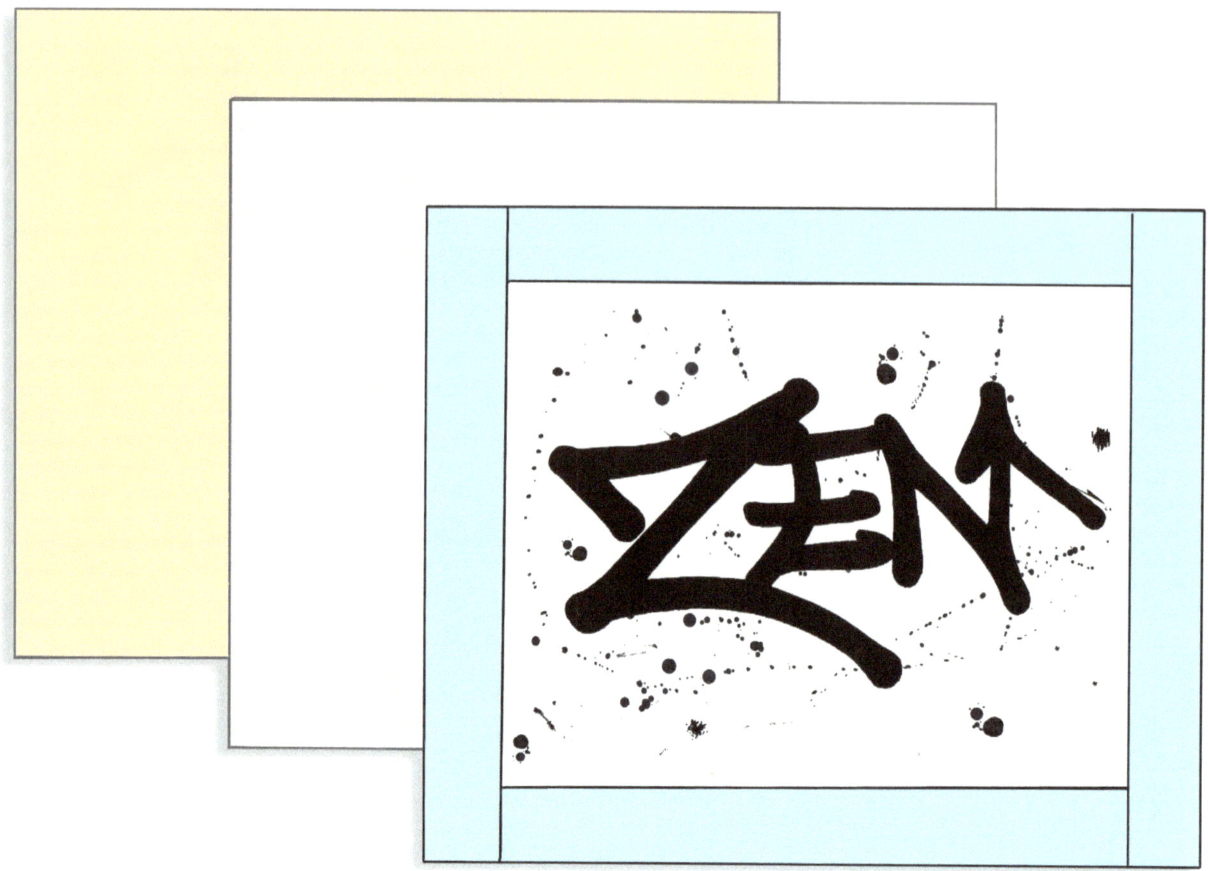

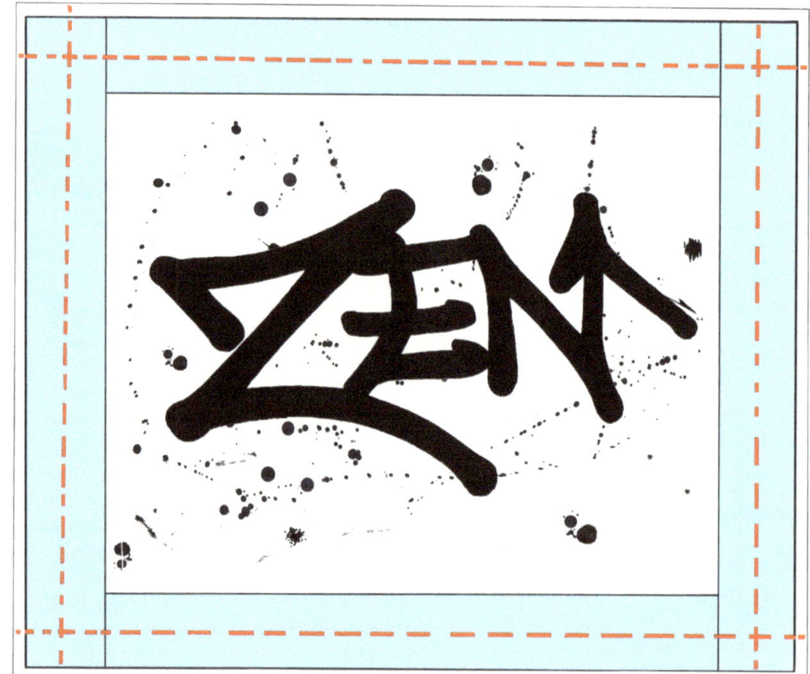

6. Sandwich the top piece, batting, and backing together with the batting on the inside. Pin with safety pins. Baste through all three layers with a brightly colored thread to hold the layers together. Remove safety pins.

7. Place the quilt top into a quilt hoop. Hand quilt along the edges of the painted tag with a thread color that matches the paint (e.g. black paint, black thread). Double or triple the thread so that it won't break. A straight running stitch is all you need to do. Outline the whole tag, pulling your stitches flat.

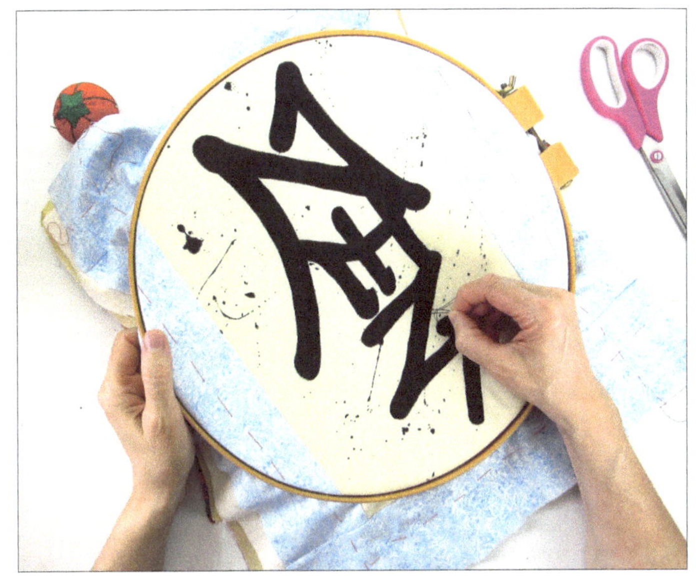

8. Take the quilt out of the hoop and lay it down flat on your table. Mark a second stitching line with a water-erasable quilter's pencil about 1/4" away from the first row of stitching. Put the quilt back in the hoop and hand quilt on this second line using a color that is closer to the color of the fabric. Repeat process.

9. Sew continuous lines of stitching around the outside of the tag. Vary the thread colors. Your quilting lines can go in any direction and be as far away from each other as you like. Stitch up to the edge of the border, then knot on the backside. Make sure all knots and thread ends are on the back of the quilt. You will be covering this back with an additional back piece in the final stage so don't worry about the back looking messy. You can quilt a design on the border, too, if you like.

Suggestions For Where To Place Quilting Lines:

FIRST ROW
Edge of paint

SECOND ROW
1/4" away from edge of paint

THIRD ROW
3/4" away from edge of paint

FOURTH ROW
1 1/2" away from edge of paint

BORDER - optional

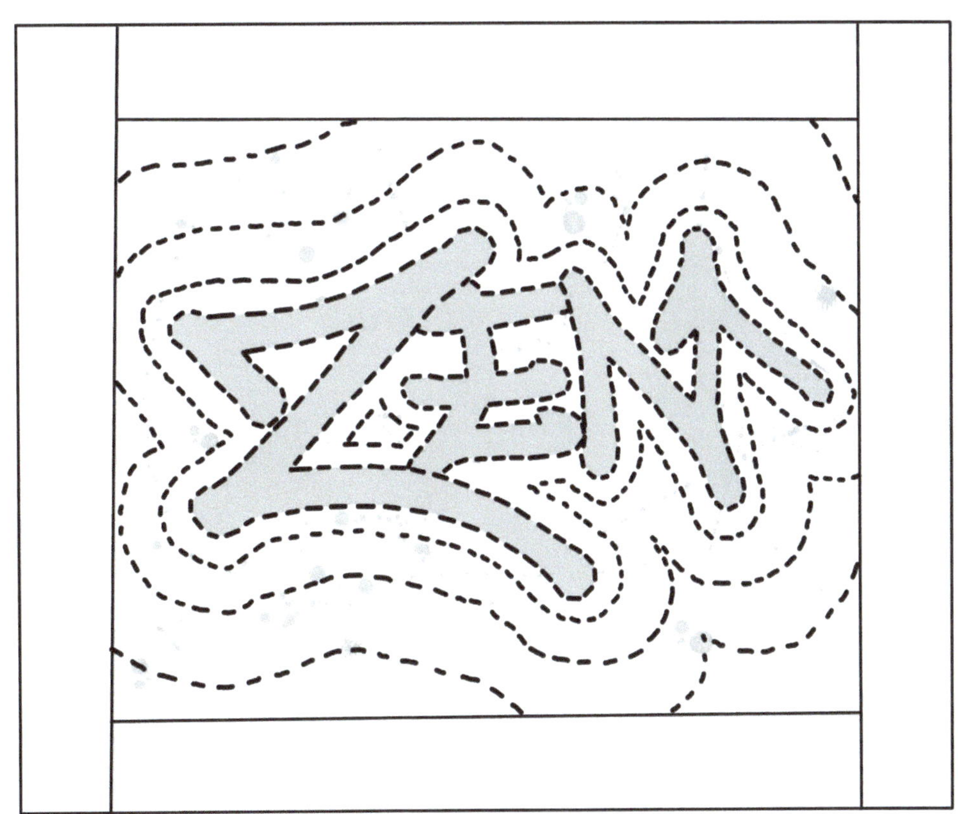

10. When quilting is complete, wipe off the pencil lines with a damp washcloth.

11. Remove basting stitches. Turn the quilt to the backside and press. Trim batting and backing edges even with raw edges of quilt top.

12. Cut a new piece of backing fabric the same size as the quilt top.

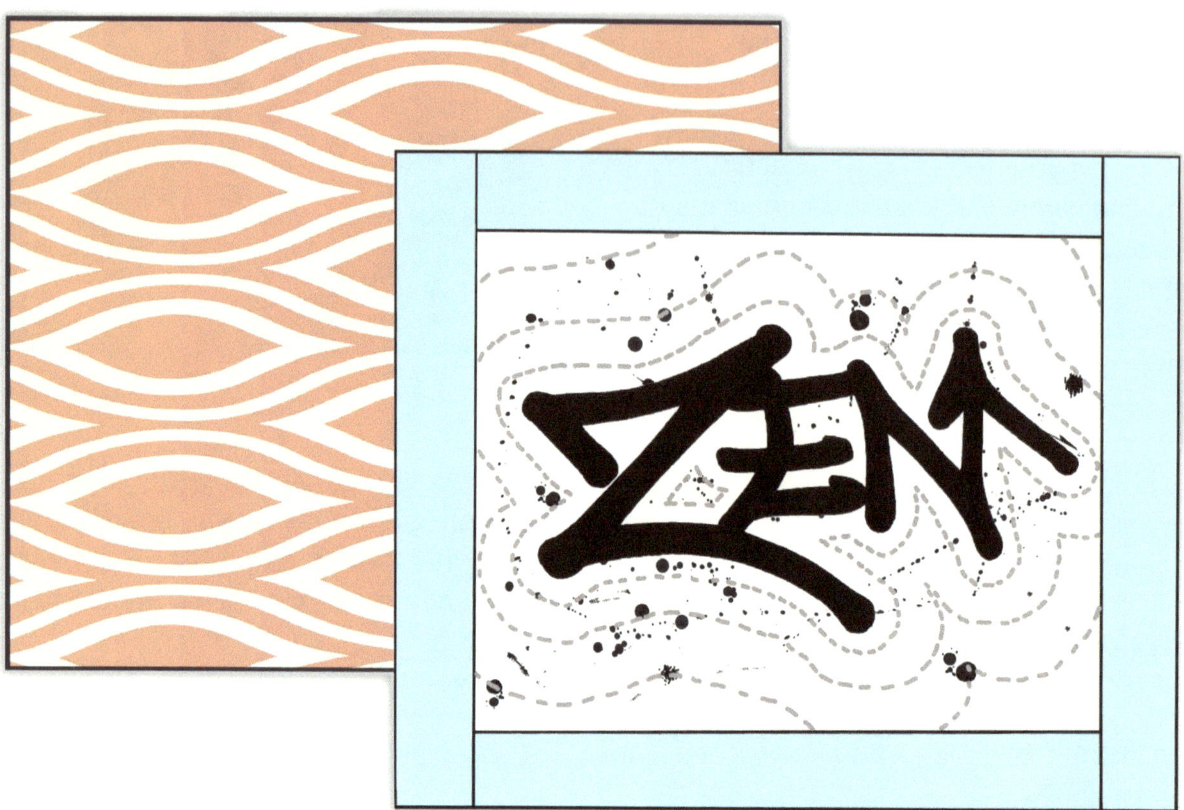

13. Lay the backing fabric down on a flat surface, wrong side up. Place the quilt top with the right side facing up on top of the backing fabric. Pin through all layers with safety pins. Baste the layers together. Remove the pins.

NOTE: This additional backing piece will hide your quilting knots and loose thread ends inside the quilt.

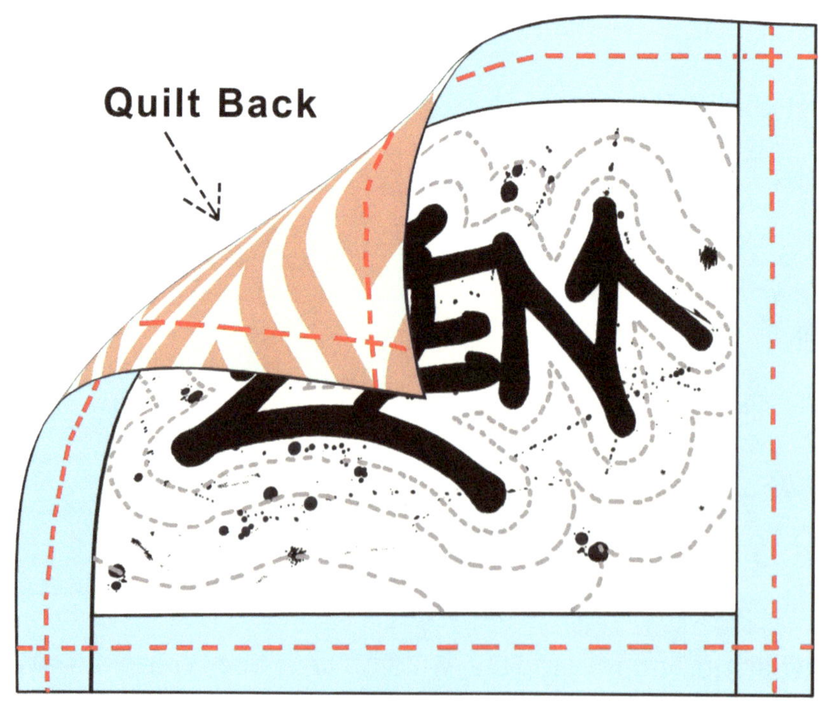

BINDING THE QUILT EDGE WITH BIAS TAPE

I prefer to start on the quilt sides, but you can begin binding anywhere on the edge of the quilt.

1. Cut a piece of bias tape one inch longer than the side width of the quilt. On the quilt front, line up the raw edge of the bias tape with the raw edge of the quilt. Pin, baste, then stitch the bias tape to the quilt with a 1/4" seam allowance. Use a thread color that matches the bias tape.

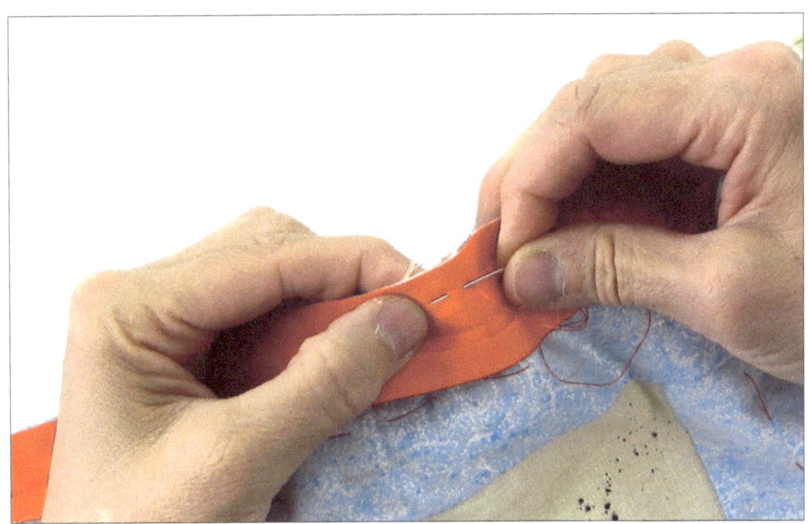

2. Fold the bias tape up, over, and to the back of the quilt, covering the stitching lines and raw edges.

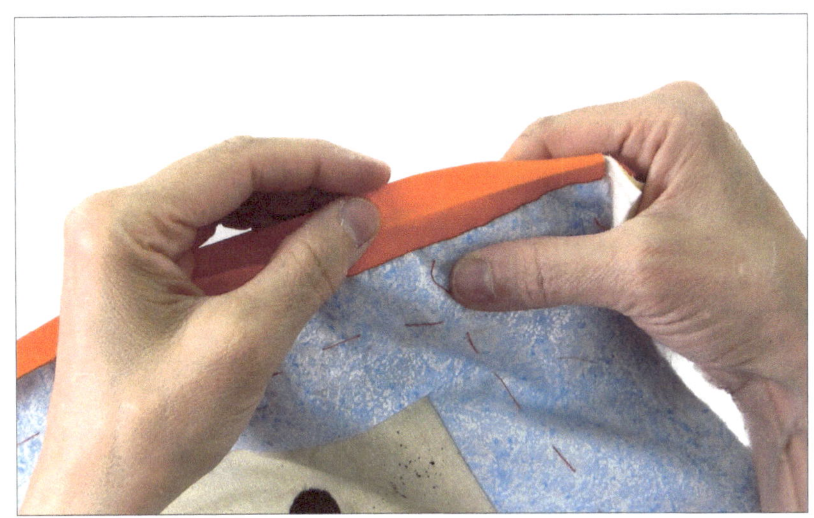

3. Lay the bias tape flat against the quilt back with the raw edges tucked inside the tape. Pin, baste, and slipstitch the bias tape in place on the quilt back. Trim excess bias tape at the side ends.

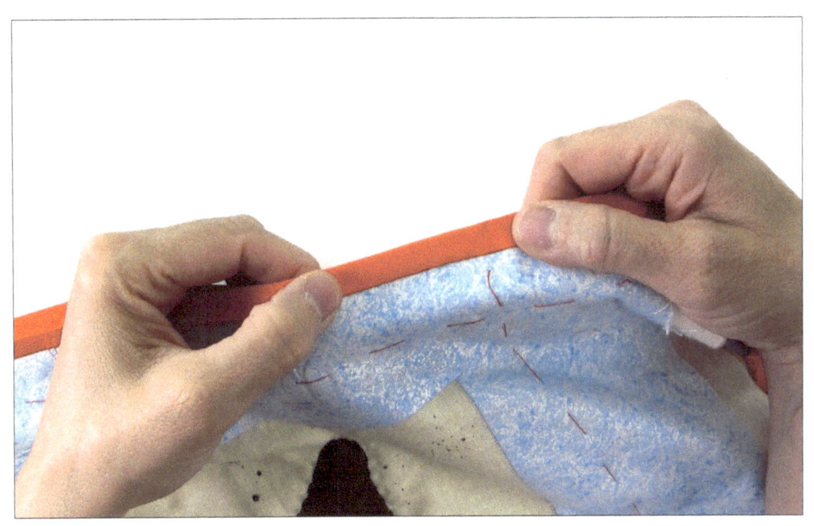

4. Cut another piece of bias tape and sew onto the other side of the quilt following the same steps 1-3.

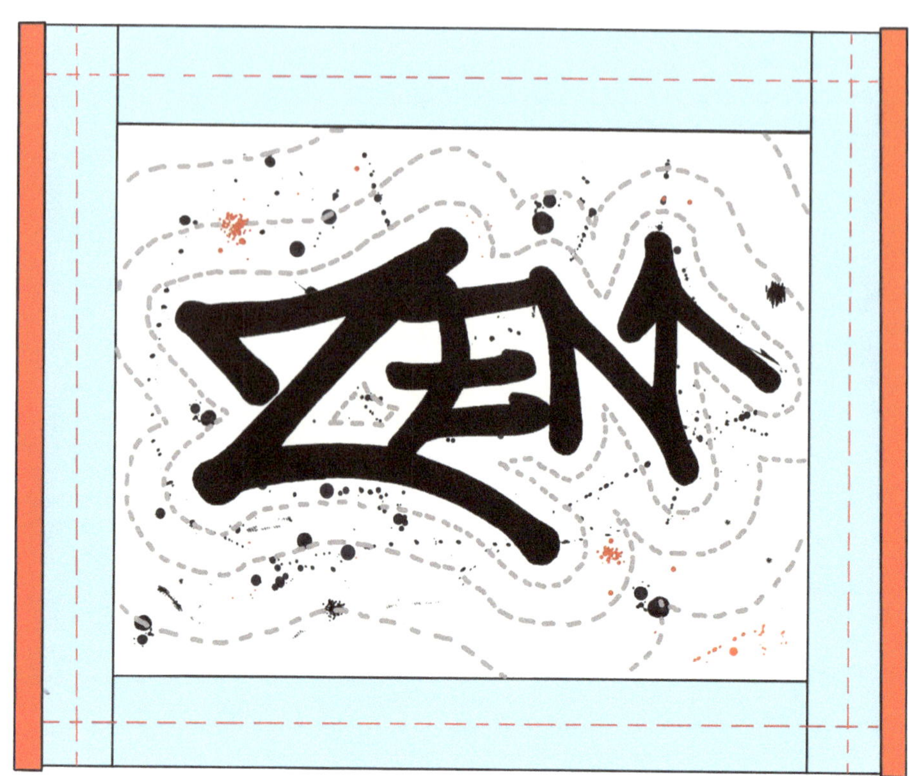

OPTION: You might like to splash a few extra drops of paint on the tag design to match the color of the bias tape. This will tie the whole quilt together visually.

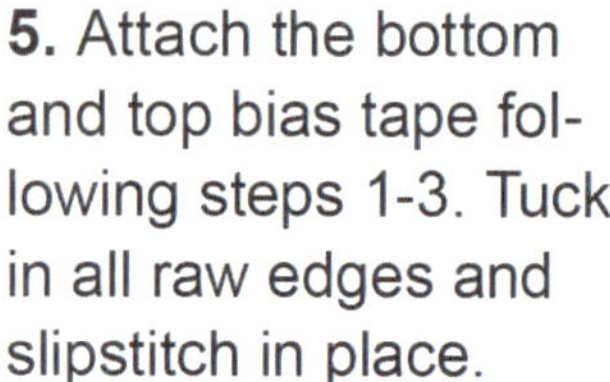

5. Attach the bottom and top bias tape following steps 1-3. Tuck in all raw edges and slipstitch in place.

NOTE: Adding the top bias tape last will give the quilt a finished look.

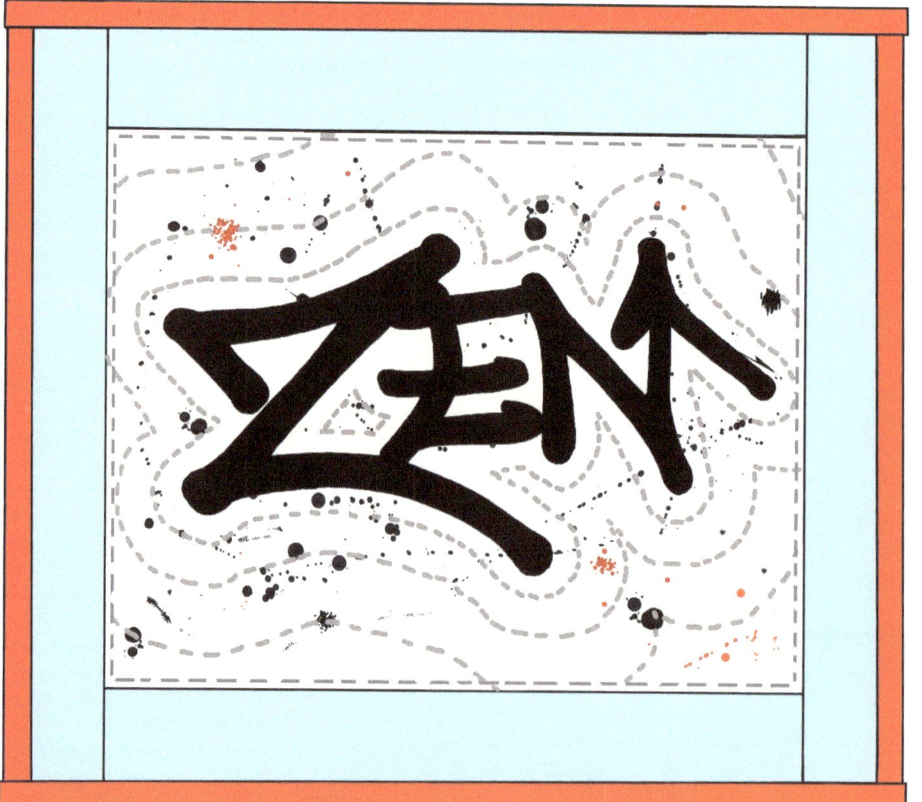

6. Quilt around the edges of the inner panel through all layers. This will help to bond all of the layers together and stabilize the quilt. Remove basting.

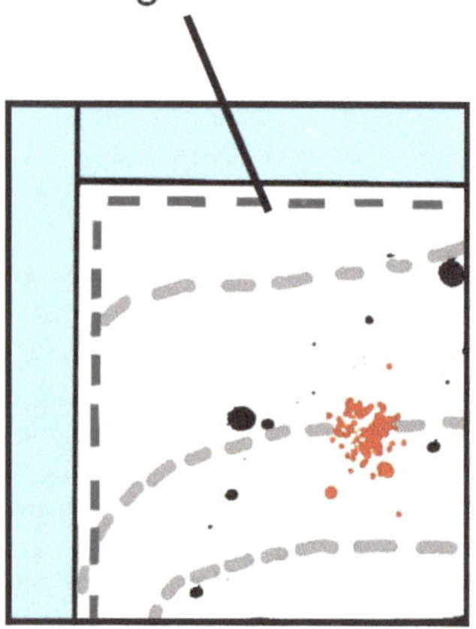

HANGING YOUR MINI QUILT

NOTE: Don't be concerned if your quilts aren't perfect rectangles or squares. I used a bit of Photoshop magic throughout this book to make my quilts appear more symmetrical than they are.

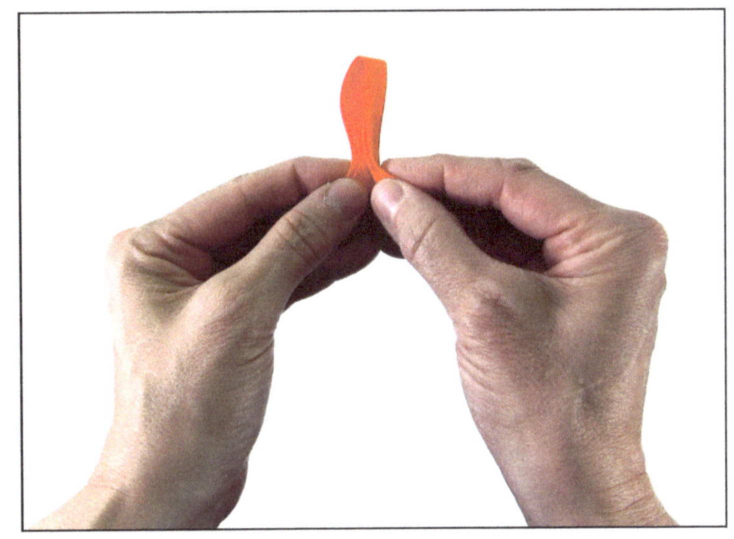

1. Cut five strips of bias tape 4 1/2" long each for loops to hang the quilt. Fold each stripe in half and tack the bottom edges together with a stitch of thread in a matching color.

2. Cut a wooden dowel one inch longer than the width of the quilt. Paint with watery brown acrylic paint (watery paint simulates wood stain). When dry varnish with semi-gloss or high-gloss varnish.

3. Sew the loops onto the top edge of the quilt along the bias tape at the quilt back. Space them evenly apart. Insert the rod into the loops and hang in a spot where you can admire your creation. Make as many copies of your mini quilt as you like.

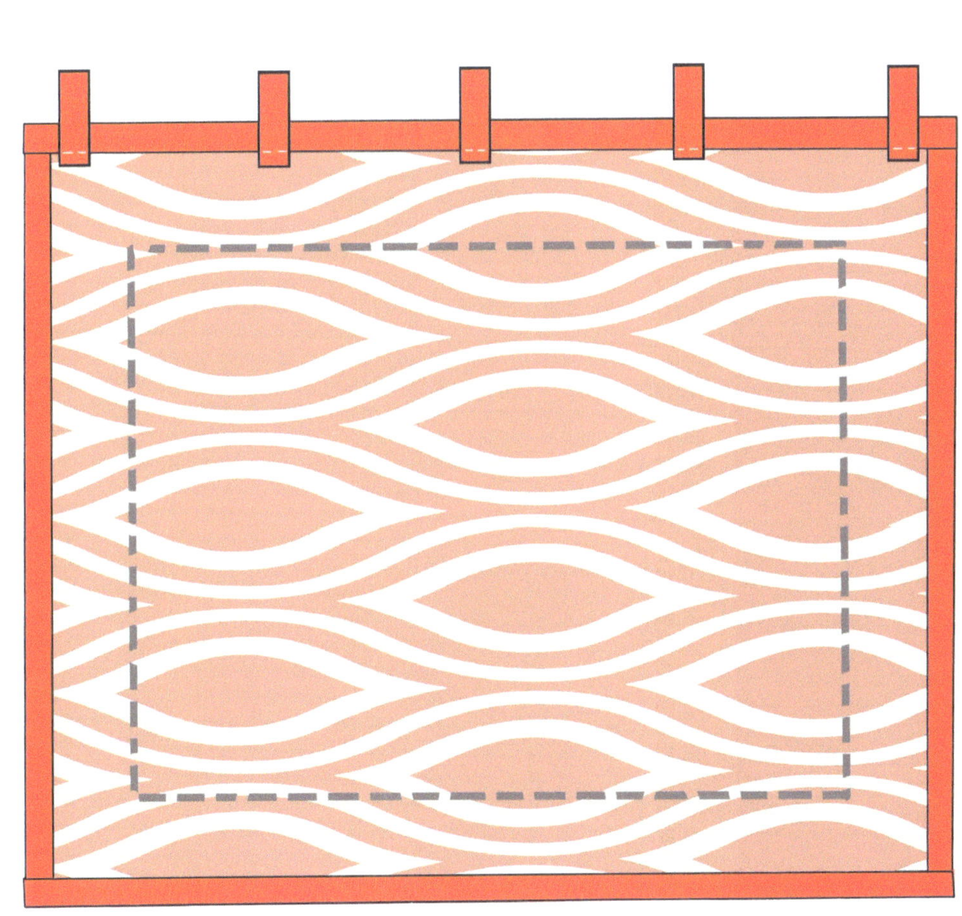

BACK VIEW

Congratulations! You have successfully completed your graffiti tag mini quilt.

www.ingramcontent.com/pod-product-compliance
Lightning Source LLC
LaVergne TN
LVHW070153110826
845147LV00002B/391

* 9 7 8 0 9 9 0 4 3 8 1 7 5 *